Gilles Deleuze's
Empiricism and
Subjectivity

Leopards break into the temple and drink all the sacrificial vessels dry; it keeps happening; in the end, it can be calculated in advance and is incorporated into the ritual.

Franz Kafka

Gilles Deleuze's Empiricism and Subjectivity

A Critical Introduction and Guide

JON ROFFE

EDINBURGH
University Press

Edinburgh University Press is one of the leading university presses in the UK. We publish academic books and journals in our selected subject areas across the humanities and social sciences, combining cutting-edge scholarship with high editorial and production values to produce academic works of lasting importance. For more information visit our website: www.edinburghuniversitypress.com

Edinburgh University Press Ltd
The Tun – Holyrood Road, 12(2f) Jackson's Entry, Edinburgh EH8 8PJ

Typeset in 11.5/15 Adobe Sabon by
IDSUK (DataConnection) Ltd, and
printed and bound in Great Britain by
CPI Group (UK) Ltd, Croydon CR0 4YY

A CIP record for this book is available from the British Library

ISBN 978 1 4744 0582 9 (hardback)
ISBN 978 1 4744 0584 3 (webready PDF)
ISBN 978 1 4744 0583 6 (paperback)
ISBN 978 1 4744 0585 0 (epub)

Contents

Acknowledgements

My thanks go to Carol Macdonald for talking me into writing this book, and for her patience during the distended period of time it took me to make good on the promise. I dedicate this book to Virginia, who kept me still and sane enough to write it.

I would also like to acknowledge the support of the Faculty of Arts and Social Sciences at the University of New South Wales for supporting the publication of this work, and Haydie Gooder for preparing the excellent index.

Note on References

In what follows, Deleuze's book will be referred to each time with a pair of page numbers, the French original followed by Constantin Boundas's English translation – for example (ES 23/21). I have frequently modified the translation, but whenever the change turns around a significant point, a note will be appended. Whenever a single page number appears, it should be taken to refer just to the French original, with the exception of references that use lower-case Roman numerals. These indicate the preface to the English translation that Deleuze contributed in 1991.

Boundas has done a great service to readers of *Empiricism and Subjectivity* by tracking down the original English passages in Hume's work that Deleuze cites in André Leroy's translation, allowing for an easy location of these texts. Here, I will follow the now standard procedure of citing from the Clarendon Edition of the Works of David Hume. References to *A Treatise of Human Nature* will take the form (T 1.3.1.1), indicating the book, chapter, section and paragraph respectively. References to *Enquiry concerning Human Understanding* will refer to section and paragraph (e.g. EHU 2.6); the *Enquiry concerning the Principles of Morals* will invoke section, part and paragraph (EPM 3.1.4).

Preface

Gilles Deleuze published his first book *Empiricism and Subjectivity: An Essay on Hume's Theory of Human Nature* in 1953, the year that he turned twenty-eight.[1] There is a pleasing symmetry here: David Hume was the same age when the first two books of his precocious masterpiece *A Treatise of Human Nature* (1739) initially appeared.[2]

A book on David Hume might seem an unusual, even bizarre, choice for a young French philosopher, educated at the height of the dynastic rule of *les trois H* in French philosophy – Hegel, Husserl, Heidegger. Even today, you would have to extend the list of influential Hs in French philosophy for a very long time before Hume's name would appear on it. The least we can say is that Deleuze's disregard for intellectual fashion and what would today, even more than then, pass for sensible career decisions was already in full flower in his philosophical youth.

This is not to say that the work had no precursors or patrons in Deleuze's milieu. Deleuze occasionally refers to the influence of Jean Wahl, whose Preface to *Vers le concret* (1932) includes a brief remark about Hume's empiricism that strikingly resembles the line of argument that will appear in *Empiricism and Subjectivity*. Despite the fact that Wahl's doctoral thesis *The Pluralist Philosophies of England and America* (1920) explicitly marginalises Hume's contribution,[3] Deleuze will write that he 'had the ability to make us think, in French, things which were very new'.[4] But *Empiricism and Subjectivity* is not dedicated to Wahl but to one of Deleuze's teachers and a champion of the young idiosyncrat, the towering Hegelian Jean Hyppolite – 'in sincere and respectful homage'. This dedication is something of a riddle, and one that we will later try to solve.

*

The translator's introduction by Constantin Boundas is the first text on *Empiricism and Subjectivity* that connects the book to a range of themes prominent in Deleuze's mature work, but the truth is that there is at first blush little in either Hume's philosophy or Deleuze's account of it that directly resembles his later, more well-known works. Readers of these works are likely to find themselves confronted to some degree by the foreign character of Deleuze's argument. Conversely, the Hume that lives on in contemporary, predominantly analytic, Anglo-American philosophy departments is not easily recognisable in his Deleuzian portrait either. This book hopes to present an account of *Empiricism and Subjectivity* that will be of interest and illumination to readers coming from either direction. That said, the aim here is not to set up a comparison between Deleuze's reading and those prominent in the Anglo-American tradition from Beattie to Baier. The reader familiar with this trajectory will nevertheless find it gradually appear in the discussions of naturalism and Hume's moral thought that will emerge as we tease out Deleuze's argument. Neither is the goal of this book the connecting up of ideas in *Empiricism and Subjectivity* and those we find later in his work. Readers interested in either or both of these approaches will find them in Jeffrey Bell's *Deleuze's Hume: Philosophy, Culture and the Scottish Enlightenment*. Again, though, and particularly in the later chapters, a few points will emerge in passing that address the way in which Deleuze's reading of Hume might open onto his later work.

Finally, the presentation that follows will not put Deleuze's Hume in the docks of comparative scholarship. Judging the fidelity of his reading of Hume is not the goal. No, my aim here is more modest: to schematically present the argument of Deleuze's little text. His writing, here as elsewhere, is remarkably dense. Rarely does he repeat a point, and rarely does he need more than a page to present even complex arguments. At the same time, his interpretation of Hume, though brief, is remarkably wide-ranging. While the *Treatise* is his central reference, he ranges across the whole of Hume's writings, including the two *Enquiries*, the *Dialogues concerning Natural Religion*, and his political and economic essays.[5] And while he does not dwell on the content of Hume's history of England, he does make an important place for it in his inclusive reading of Humean thought.

We can add to this the fact that, as is often the case in Deleuze's works, the order of argumentation is unusual and, to some extent at least, misleading. The logic of this order is certainly present in *Empiricism and Subjectivity*, but it is woven through the book, and only appears to the reader once a certain level of comprehension is already gained. Consequently, to replay in full Deleuze's reading of Hume in its richness and idiosyncrasy would require a book significantly longer than the original, and the one in your possession is already (embarrassingly) longer than it should be. What follows is thus a schematic and thematic treatment. Rather than proceed in a linear fashion, each of the following chapters focuses on one of the major topics that Deleuze discusses. They are ordered to show that what is really at issue in the book is a series of ramifying problems that emerge once we take Hume's starting point seriously and follow through its consequences. Following this series will carry us from the classical problem of justifying beliefs about the world to the definition of subjectivity that is at the heart of Deleuze's reading. The last two chapters present, like the two termini of a pendulum's swing, empiricism and Kantianism, the two poles of *Empiricism and Subjectivity*, and the two orientations that frame Deleuze's portrait of Hume.

Before we begin the discussion of this, Deleuze's least-read work, a final question beckons: really, why write a book about it at all? While it hardly 'fell *dead-born from the press*',[6] it has surely garnered less attention than any other. The necessity for secondary work in philosophy is always questionable, and this book is more questionable than most. This very unfamiliarity on the part of Deleuze's readers of *Empiricism and Subjectivity* is one excuse for its publication, of course. There is also the two-fold conviction I have already implied: that, on the one hand, readers of Hume in the analytic tradition would gain much from an engagement with Deleuze's little study; and that readers familiar with Deleuze can learn a great deal about thematics that would later become, sometimes by way of a complex of hidden conceptual tunnels, prominent in his more famous works. More profoundly, though, to lead someone to a great work of philosophy is never a waste of time. It is a pleasure to dwell on this book of Deleuze's, and a pleasure to explain, in all of these unnecessary words, why it continues to resonate in the mind, like the ever-expanding halo of echoes that make the repetition of a single bowed note of a cello into its own proper world.

NOTES

1. Gilles Deleuze, *Empiricisme et Subjectivité* (Paris: Presses universitaires de France, 1953), translated as *Empiricism and Subjectivity: An Essay on Hume's Theory of Human Nature*, trans. Constantin Boundas (New York: Columbia University Press, 1991).
2. David Hume, *A Treatise of Human Nature* (*The Clarendon Edition of the Works of David Hume*), ed. David Fate Norton and Mary J. Norton (Oxford: Oxford University Press, 2011). The date of original publication has been the object of some disagreement. In listing (January) 1739, I am following David Fate Norton's introduction to the *Treatise*, which is supported by superior historical data (T i9, i11).
3. The following sentiment is the kindest that appears there: 'Hume does not fully satisfy us nowadays; but if we must correct him,

let us do so while we remain his disciples, and not have recourse to the "evasions and artifices of Kant"' (Jean Wahl, *The Pluralist Philosophies of England and America*, trans. Fred Rothwell (London: Open Court, 1925), 89). Ironically, it is just these 'evasions and artifices' that will be key for Deleuze, both in *Empiricism and Subjectivity* and more generally. See the final chapter below on this point.

4. Gilles Deleuze and Claire Parnet, *Dialogues*, trans. Hugh Tomlinson and Barbara Habberjam (New York: Columbia University Press, 1987), 57–8.

5. David Hume, *An Enquiry concerning Human Understanding*, ed. Tom L. Beauchamp (Oxford: Oxford University Press, 2006); *An Enquiry concerning the Principles of Morals*, ed. Tom L. Beauchamp (Oxford: Oxford University Press, 2006); *Dialogues concerning Natural Religion*, ed. Richard Popkin (Indianapolis: Hackett Publishing, 1988); *Essays: Moral, Political and Literary* (New York: Cosimo, 2006).

6. David Hume, 'My Own Life', in *The Cambridge Companion to Hume*, ed. David Fate Norton (Cambridge: Cambridge University Press, 1993), 352.

1

Beyond Kant's Hume

Perhaps the single most well-known passage in the work of David Hume is a discussion of causality that he sets in the context of a convivial game of billiards:

> When I see, for instance, a Billiard-ball moving in a straight line towards another; [. . .] may I not conceive, that a hundred different events might as well follow from the cause? May not both these balls remain at absolute rest? May not the first ball return in a straight line, or leap off from the second in any line or direction? All these suppositions are consistent and conceivable. Why then should we give the preference to one, which is no more consistent or conceivable than the rest? All our reasonings *a priori* will never be able to show us any foundation for this preference. (EHU 4.25)

Hume is often taken to be the greatest of British philosophers. An extremely broad-reaching thinker, both precocious and prolific, his work in philosophy, history, religion and economics has had an immeasurable influence in the history of philosophy, on both sides of the Channel. It is impossible to write a book about Hume without recalling Bertrand Russell's infamous words, 'There is a peculiarly painful chamber inhabited solely by philosophers who have refuted Hume. These philosophers, though in Hell, have not learned wisdom.'[1] No less memorable is Schopenhauer's claim in *The World as Will and Representation*:

'In every page of David Hume, there is more to be learned than from Hegel's, Herbart's and Schleiermacher's complete philosophical works.'[2] His treatment of causality and his more general consideration of the nature of conceptual thinking led Charles Darwin and Albert Einstein, among others, to proclaim him a decisive precursor.

And yet ... when Hume is taught in undergraduate philosophy courses the world over, when his intellectual legacy is invoked, his vast reach is often reduced down to a single argument. To find assertions of Hume's minimalism as a philosopher is in no way uncommon.[3] This single argument concerns what is known as the problem of induction, and the discussion of billiards cited above presents it very clearly.

There is no need to be a crack billiards player to conclude from the direction of the white ball what will happen when it hits the red ball on the table: the white ball moves accordingly. Hume's point is that *in fact* any certainty we might feel about this is never justified. It is equally conceivable that the red ball may leap up into the air, stay still, with or without the white ball going back the way it came, or an innumerable number of other things. We might be tempted to respond to these logical possibilities by saying, 'This is just not how cause and effect works in the physical world.' To this assertion, Hume asks a simple question: what is the source of our knowledge of causal relations? Because what we actually see when we watch billiard balls move around is not cause and effect, but only one movement after another. Causality itself is not an object of experience; what I actually see is what Hume calls *constant conjunction*. The white ball moves, then stops, and the red ball moves off.

'But,' we might respond, 'the red ball always goes in the pot when it's hit in the right way – isn't this evidence that there is an objective order of cause and effect in play?' For Hume, the answer to this question is a clear 'no'. In fact, we cannot say that the red ball always behaves in this way, because we can never experience all of the relevant cases. All we really know is that all of our experiences of billiards conform to this *so far*. But because all I ever experience is constant conjunction, and lacking the possession of a universal law of moving bodies, I am never in a position to say more than, 'This is how it's always gone in my experience.' I have literally no justification to pass from this finite set of occurrences to the assertion of a general law of nature. More generally again, 'All our reasonings *a priori* will never be able to show us any foundation for this preference' (EHU 4.25).

It should be clear that this conclusion is not restricted to causality, but rather concerns any and all claims that I might make about reality as it is beyond the limited range of my experiences. In Hume's words, 'there can be no *demonstrative* arguments to prove, *that those instances, of which we have had no experience, resemble those, of which we have had experience*' (T 1.3.6.5). It should also be clear, taken in isolation and on its own terms, this conclusion spectacularly closes down any further investigation. It may be that there is a hell for philosophers who have thought they have refuted Hume – but the success of this version of Hume is its own kind of hell for philosophy.

KANT'S HUME

This reduction of Hume's thought to the single problematic of induction is first to be found in the work of Immanuel Kant, who famously – if somewhat misleadingly, and more ambiguously than it is often reported – claimed that 'the remembrance of *David Hume* was the very first thing that many years ago first interrupted my dogmatic slumber and gave a completely different direction to my researches in the field of speculative philosophy'.[4] The following passage from the *Critique of Pure Reason* is emblematic:

> The famous David Hume was one of these geographers of human reason [. . .] He dwelt primarily on the principle of causality, and quite rightly remarked about that that one could not base its truth (Indeed not even the objective validity of the concept of an efficient cause in general) on any Insight **at** all . . .[5]

Early in the second edition of the *Critique*, he writes:

> David Hume [. . .] stopped with the synthetic proposition of the connection of the effect with its cause (*Principium causalitatii*), believing himself to have brought out that such an *a priori* proposition is entirely impossible, and according to his inferences everything that we call metaphysics would come down to a mere delusion of an alleged insight of reason into that which has in fact merely been borrowed from experience and from habit has taken on the appearance of necessity . . .[6]

Most succinctly, Kant will write in the *Prolegomena* that 'the concept of cause [is] *Hume's* problematic concept (this, his *crux metaphysicorum*)'.[7]

Now, Kant's lack of first-hand familiarity with Hume's philosophy, and his misunderstandings of it, are well established. A German translation of the *Treatise of Human Nature* was first published in 1790, years after these passages were composed, and many years after Hume's wake-up call that Kant 'recollects' having taken place around 1772.[8] It would seem that his knowledge of the induction argument came by way of a translation of James Beattie's *Essay on the Nature and Immutability of Truth*, which discusses Hume at length, and which was published in German in 1772. Beattie, however, was a critic of Hume's work, and a ham-fisted one at that. In reading Kant's work on Hume, we should as a result keep in mind Hume's own opinion of his paraphraser (who he called the 'biggotted, silly fellow, Beattie'[9]) and of his account of Hume's philosophy ('there is no truth in it; it is a horrible large lie *in octavo*'[10]). At the very least, we should take Kant's reading of Hume with a large grain of salt.

However, it would be a mistake to see this insistence of the problem of induction as beginning and ending with Kant, for in fact Kant's approach to Hume's thought is the beginning of the major tradition in Hume scholarship up until the present day. Very recently indeed, for example, we read the following:

The difficulty which we have just identified is a familiar philosophical problem – it is known as 'Hume's problem' [. . .] What is this problem? In its traditional version, it can be formulated as follows: is it possible to establish that the same effects will always follow from the same causes *ceteris paribus*, i.e. all other things being equal? In other words, can one establish that in identical circumstances, future successions of phenomena will always be identical to previous successions? The question raised by Hume concerns our capacity to demonstrate the necessity of the causal connection.[11]

The text is from Quentin Meillassoux's celebrated *After Finitude*, and is extracted from a chapter entitled (what else?) 'Hume's Problem'.

'WHY WOULD THE EMPIRICIST SAY THAT?'

It is certainly true that Hume's work is devoted in no small part to epistemological questions, and even the discussion of probability that arises on the basis of his particular form of scepticism about cause and effect relations is widespread, appearing, for example, in his famous essay on miracles. For Deleuze, though, to see Hume through this lens is to be led into a near-total misreading. In one of a few fiery passages in *Empiricism and Subjectivity*, he writes that

> The classical definition of empiricism proposed by the Kantian tradition is this: empiricism is the theory according to which knowledge not only begins with experience but is derived from it. But why would the empiricist say that? And as the result of which question? [. . .] the definition is in no way satisfactory [. . .] In short, it seems impossible to define empiricism as a theory according to which knowledge derives from experience. (ES 121/107–8)

The problem here is twofold. On the one hand, for Deleuze Hume's thought dramatically overflows specifically epistemological concerns. On the other, and more interestingly, Deleuze is asserting here that the general orienting question that Kant's

Hume poses is *not an empiricist question*. Implicit here is a conception of the nature of philosophy that we shall examine in detail later. The central point though is this: any characterisation of a philosophy must begin by presenting its defining problems. If we begin our reading with 'Hume's problem', as it is conceived in the wake of Kant, we will only ever arrive at a partial, mutilated picture of what is really at stake.

Now, despite the force of these words, Deleuze's reading of Hume does not aim to entirely reject this Kantian heritage. Instead, his goal is to situate the epistemological strains of Hume's philosophy within the broader context of his thought as a whole. In keeping with his general methodology for reading other philosophers, this broader context is presented by Deleuze as a wide-ranging yet coherent system, in which all of the parts fit together.

TWO WAYS OF BEGINNING WITH HUMAN NATURE

What then *is* Hume's problem for Deleuze? What is the point of view that will allow for the integration of the epistemological enquiries into a broader framework? In fact, it is signalled already in the very first words of the *Treatise*:

> 'Tis evident, that all the sciences have a relation, greater or less, to human nature; and that however wide any of them may seem to run from it, they still return back by one passage or another. Even mathematics, Natural Philosophy, and Natural Religion, are in some measure dependent on the science of Man; since they lie under the cognisance of men, and are judged of by their powers and faculties [. . .] And, as the science of man is the only solid foundation for the other sciences, so the only solid foundation we can give to this science itself must be laid on experience and observation. (T Introduction 4)

In essence, there are two ways of taking this opening move of Hume's. We can take it, on the one hand, as a negative or exclusively critical point. Hume is asserting, on this view, that direct knowledge of the world is impossible, because it arrives through the filter of human nature. And given that we have no independent point of view, there is no way to abstract out this filtering. We find ourselves in the cul-de-sac of the problem of induction.

On the other hand we can read Hume as insisting on the starting point of a constructive project, and move in precisely the opposite direction. If human nature grounds the activity of science, the first question that presents itself is clearly 'what is human nature?' It is this approach that Deleuze takes. The subtitle of *Empiricism and Subjectivity* is 'An Essay on Hume's Theory of Human Nature [*Essai sur la Nature Humaine selon Hume*]', and its first sentence reads: 'Hume proposes the creation of a science of humanity, but what is really his fundamental project?' (ES 1/21). The answer to this question, in all of its aspects, constitutes the purpose of Deleuze's study. What is human nature for Hume?

It is at this point that another of Hume's famous *topoi* might spring to mind for readers with even a passing familiarity with his work: his attack on the belief in personal identity. Hume deploys the same method here as he does in relation to cause and effect. I encounter the world of things, which makes the impressions on me that, taken as a whole, we call experience.[12] All of my ideas are copies of these impressions (simple ideas), or composites of these copies (complex ideas). Now, here is the thing:

> There are some philosophers, who imagine we are every moment intimately conscious of what we call our SELF; that we feel its existence and its continuance in existence; and are certain, beyond the evidence of any demonstration, both of its perfect identity and simplicity. (T 1.4.61)

Hume's question here is simply this: what genuine evidence do we have for the existence of this self? '[F]rom what impression could this idea [of the self] be derived?' (T 1.4.61). Since all ideas arise from sensory encounters with the world, which encounters can we enlist in our proof of the idea of the self? If we really do introspect, as Descartes' meditator does, what do we find?

> [W]hen I enter most intimately into what I call myself, I always stumble on some particular perception or other, of heat or cold, light or shade, love or hatred, pain or pleasure. I never can catch myself at any time without a perception, and never can observe any thing but the perception. (T 1.4.6.3)

In other words, I *am not* – I am not a person, a unified and simple being who *has* perceptions (and here by 'perception' Hume just means the contents of thought; more on this terminology in the next chapter). Everything I actually experience tells me instead that thought is composed *exclusively* of perceptions, and that there is no self at all to whom they belong. Hume's discussion here is more nuanced than it is sometimes taken to be, but the upshot is as straightforward as it is famous: subjectivity is

> nothing but a bundle or collection of different perceptions, which succeed each other with an inconceivable rapidity, and are in a perpetual flux and movement [. . .] The mind is a kind of theatre, where several perceptions successively make their appearance; pass, repass, glide away, and mingle in an infinite variety of postures and situations. (T 1.4.6.4)

This discussion seems to lead us back to Kant's minimalist Hume; it certainly seems to answer the question 'what is human nature?' in a radically deflationary manner. What we are is a bundle of perceptions, and no more. But this is hardly the whole story. Despite the fact that we have no reason to think from experience that there is any such thing as personal identity, we are nonetheless moral, political, amorous, critical and believing subjects. We infer conclusions and rationally examine them; we own property, we follow and break laws, and we create and modify social institutions – all of these are facts too. So the real question once more will be a positive, constructive question. If we go back again to Deleuze's opening remarks, they continue as follows:

> Hume proposes the creation of a science of humanity, but what is really his fundamental project? [. . .] Hume's project entails the *substitution of a psychology of the mind by a psychology of the mind's affections.* The constitution of a psychology of the mind is not at all possible, since this psychology cannot find in its object the required constancy or universality; only a psychology of affections will be capable of constituting the true science of humanity. (ES 1/21)

Since there is no *natural* or given human nature, the constitution of a science of humanity cannot take this nature as its object. 'The mind is not nature, nor does it have a nature' (ES 3/22). This approach is what Deleuze will throughout the book call the psychological approach, the approach that falls under the heading of 'a psychology of the mind'. In its place, Hume's new science of humanity will have to take as its object the ensemble of perceptions themselves and the various formations they enter into, and will account for the whole range of human experiences on this basis. It is this that is the properly 'empiricist' approach adopted by Hume.

Consequently, Deleuze will frame his constructive reading of Hume in the following way: 'By itself and in itself, the mind is not nature; it is not the object of science. Hence the question that will preoccupy Hume is this: *how does the mind become human nature?*' (ES 2/22). Later, we will see why Deleuze will also want to claim that empiricism, as a philosophical problematic, also has the problem of subjectivity as its locus.

There is also a further extremely interesting problem that arises once we take on board Hume's sceptical method, and at the same time consider the way the mind actually functions. The question is this: since we are just an ensemble of perceptions, why is it that we nonetheless attribute personal identity to ourselves and others? Though it is a 'by mistake we ascribe to it an identity' (T 1.4.6.7), we still need to ask the further and more fundamental question: 'What then gives us so great a propension to ascribe an identity to these successive perceptions, and to suppose ourselves possest of an invariable and uninterrupted existence thro' the whole course of our lives?' (T 1.4.6.5). What is the origin of this 'fiction' (T 1.4.6.2) of the self? For, while it is a fiction, it is a *real* fiction, it is ubiquitous – and in fact, as we will see, is not limited to a belief in personal identity but also to objects in general – and it has genuine effects.

THE HUMEAN PROBLEMATIC

In fact, the most obvious feature of *Empiricism and Subjectivity* at the rhetorical level is a proliferation of questions of this kind: 'How does the mind become human nature?' (ES 2/22); 'How does a collection become a system?' (ES 3/22); 'How does the imagination become a faculty?' (ES 3/23); 'How does the imagination become human nature?' (ES 4/23); 'What factors will transform the mind?' (ES 108/98). These questions are actually more diverse than they appear, something that will become clear later. But it is nonetheless the case that Deleuze's book might be read as a kind of criminal investigation, as if it were written by a detective trying to link together the clues spread across Hume's writings into a coherent story. Once we frame Hume's work as an account of how human nature arises from an indifferent collection of perceptions in the mind, we see what kind of story Deleuze is looking to tell: if subjectivity is (in a sense yet to be seen) a product, how is it produced? How do we get from the assertion that *'The mind is identical to the ideas in the mind'* (ES 93/88) to the subject who believes and creates, the social, moral agent?

We might further frame this problematic in terms familiar to mainstream Hume scholarship. Hume's philosophy unfolds along 'two lines of diverse inspiration' (ES 9/26), and is devoted to two basic theses and two subsequent methodological convictions. On the one hand, Hume is an *atomist*. He conceives of the mind as a collection of discrete elements: impressions and ideas. This means, on the one hand, that there is no more profound level on which we might find a simple unity. Part of Hume's attack on the idea of personal identity aims to demonstrate this: there is no underlying stratum characterised by 'perfect identity and simplicity' (T 1.4.6.1), but only a plurality of different elements. As a result, Deleuze will also call Hume's commitment to atomism '*the principle of difference*' (ES 93/90).

On the other hand, Hume is also committed to the doctrine of *associationism*. In fact, it is this that marks Hume's genius and his novelty for Deleuze. If the doctrine of atomism, along with Hume's account of the origin of ideas, provides the great critical force of Humean empiricism, associationism provides it with its constructivist *élan*, since it names the aspect of Hume's thought that accounts for the advent of the coherent mind and the subject on the basis of the indifferent atomic milieu.

Consider again the billiards game, and the question of cause and effect. The critical facet of Hume's argument leads us to conclude that we have no good reason to think that there is any such thing as objective cause and effect relations in the world. But causality is not only a poorly founded fiction *in* the mind, it is also a tendency, a habit, which provides a certain order *to* the mind itself. We tend to associate things in the mind, and this tendency is a crucial part of what gives the mind order and stability, allowing us to transcend the indifferent plurality of affections. The same holds for another famous example of Hume's, the assertion that the sun will rise tomorrow (EHU 4.21). There is nothing logically problematic about either its affirmation or negation – and in fact, when Hume uses this example, he deliberately invokes the negation: '*That the sun will not rise to-morrow is no less intelligible a proposition, and implies no more contradiction than the affirmation, that it will rise*' (EHU 4.21).[13] What is problematic is the attempt to draw either conclusion from experience, since past experience has no bearing on the future at all. But, of course, this is the only evidence we can ever have. Despite the absolute explanatory gulf, nobody has ever had any trouble drawing the conclusion that the sun will come up in the morning. But why? Like the billiards case, there is and must be something that comes to bear on the mind that allows us to draw this kind of logically and evidentially illegitimate conclusion, despite its illegitimacy, something that gets us into the habit of believing what we cannot know.

THE PRINCIPLES OF HUMAN NATURE

'What factors will transform the mind?' (ES 108/98). Hume calls these factors *the principles of human nature*.[14] That one of his ultimate goals is to grasp these factors and their scope of operation is indicated in all of his major works. In the Introduction to the *Treatise*, for example, he describes his general goal as 'explaining the principles of human nature' (T Introduction 43), while early in the *Enquiry*, he insists that founding all of the sciences requires that we 'discover, at least in some degree, the secret springs and principle, by which the human mind is actuated in its operations' (EHU 1.9). The broadest trajectory of Hume's thought, on Deleuze's reading, is thus summarised in the following assertion: 'The mind, having been affected by the principles, turns now into a subject' (ES 8/26). It is these principles that explain how we pass from indifferent collection to active subjectivity.

Most of what we will examine in subsequent chapters will turn around an explanation of the nature, variety and functioning of the principles, but we can say schematically that they fall into two classes. The first are the principles of association. These principles are what give rise to the possibility of forming (relatively) reliable beliefs. To return to the billiards example, I tend to associate the white and the red balls in terms of a cause and effect relationship. This relation is, as Hume has shown, not to be found in experience itself but must be added to it by the subject. Cause and effect – one of the principles of the understanding – is *a rule of association in the mind*, not *a rule of nature discovered through experience*.

This capacity is twofold, though: the principles of association explain not only how beliefs are formed, but how the believing subject arises. The ease of transition between white and red ball on the billiards table, and the myriad other such connections, are the very flesh and bones of subjectivity. Notice too that what the principles of the understanding make possible is not knowledge but *belief*. Deleuze will often insist on the novelty of this Humean shift. In enumerating Hume's 'essential and creative contributions', Deleuze writes: 'He established the concept of *belief* and put it in the place of knowledge. He laicized belief, turning knowledge into a legitimate belief' (ES ix).

The second set of principles are the principles of the passions. While Deleuze will also deal with the famous Humean themes of sympathy, egoism, moral sentiment and the will, his overall approach to Hume's moral philosophy is oriented by structural and genetic concerns to an unusual and unorthodox degree. The most striking evidence of this is that the phrase 'the principles of the passions' never appears in Hume in these terms, and only rare and passing remarks seem to warrant its use. The passions in question, though, are the responses in the subject to pleasure and pain, responses like hope and fear, hatred and love. In turn, the principles of the passions will not be any set of rational ideals brought to bear on the messy amoral stuff of social life, but the means by which moral distinctions (between virtue and vice, for example) arise in the first place.

Even more important than this remarkable inversion, on Deleuze's view, is the fact that these principles and the moral categories that they give rise to are not subjective in the narrow sense. The very operation of the principles of the passions is necessarily extended into the social world itself, such that simple pleasures and pains are linked not just to moral values like good and bad, but to social institutions – like marriage, aesthetic taste, or property ownership – which allow them to be integrated, for the good of the society as a whole. This is why the most important effects of the principles of the passions are not moral values and a judging subject, but social institutions and an inventive subject.

Beliefs and practices, and the subject that believes and invents – such are the products of the double principles of human nature. But here already we need to add three caveats. First, as we will come to see, there is an additional class of principles, even if for the most part it is enough for the moment to recognise the nature of *Hume's solution*, and to recognise the division between the epistemic and the moral that it involves. This third class includes *habit* and *experience* as principles properly speaking.

It is important, secondly, to qualify the kind of knowledge we can have of the principles themselves. There is obviously no way for Hume to assert that they can be the object of a direct knowledge. We know, and can know, nothing about the nature of the principles as such, or anything about their origins or source (it is easy to imagine the Humean riposte: what impression corresponds to these principles you claim to know?). All that we know of the principles are their effects in the mind.

Given this, Hume's approach can seem to be a kind of precursor to the famous transcendental method first presented in Kant's *Critique of Pure Reason*, which allows us to pass from the facts of experience to their conditions of possibility. In fact, Hume is quite explicitly doing something else, and something much more straightforward: he is applying the scientific method as it had been elaborated by Newton. Hume's 'New Science' is only new with respect to its object, but its method remains the same: what is at issue is an *induction*. This is why Hume is careful to qualify what we might learn about the principles with phrases like 'in some degree', and why the method he uses to arrive at claims about them depends upon 'experience and observation' (T Introduction 7).

The final caveat concerns the relative significance of the passions and the understanding. One thing that Deleuze is particularly keen to emphasise in *Empiricism and Subjectivity* from the very first page is the primacy of the practical, the moral or the social (these are, in the end, equivalent, as we will see) in relation to epistemological concerns in Hume's thought. This is clearly in keeping with the displacement of the Kantian Hume, but is hardly controversial. The full title of the Treatise is, let us recall, *A Treatise of Human Nature: Being an Attempt to introduce the experimental Method of Reasoning into Moral Subjects.*

Hume's claims on this front are justly famous, perhaps none as much as this hallmark: 'Reason is, and ought only to be the slave of the passions, and can never pretend to any other office than to serve and obey them' (T 3.3.3.4). This, the emphasis on the practical insufficiency of reason, is central to Deleuze's reading of Hume. He will even go so far as to assert that the 'principal sentence of the *Treatise* is this: "'Tis not contrary to reason to prefer the destruction of the whole world to the scratching of my finger"' (ES 18/33, quoting T 2.3.3.6).

We will discuss in detail exactly why Hume thinks this, and its consequences for his system. For now, it is enough to see that for Deleuze, epistemic interests in Hume are always subordinated to practical and moral interests. As Deleuze puts it, 'The passions and the understanding present themselves [. . .] as two distinct parts. By itself, though, the understanding is only the process of the passions on their way to socialization' (ES 2/22).

Having noted this point, we will nonetheless begin in the next chapter with belief, and the concomitant principles of the understanding. This is not only to provide a way into Deleuze's account of Hume for readers familiar with his position on epistemological questions. It is by grasping how beliefs are produced under the rule of the principles of the understanding that we arrive at the starkest reason for their insufficiency. To invoke the title of Francisco Goya's famous etching, it is not the sleep of reason that engenders monstrous fictions for Hume, but reason itself. Our most highly developed capacity for believing and legitimating our beliefs gives rise to problems that cannot be resolved on their own grounds. The moral and the social will be the only means to modulate the spiralling descent into delirium bequeathed to us by the understanding in its full deployment.

NOTES

1. Bertrand Russell, *Nightmares of Eminent Persons, and Other Stories* (Nottingham: Spokesman, 2000), 32.
2. Arthur Schopenhauer, *The World as Will and Representation*, vol. II (Mineola, NY: Dover, 1966), 582.
3. A relatively recent example is to be found in Jerry Fodor, *Hume Variations* (Oxford: Oxford University Press, 2003).
4. Immanuel Kant, *Prolegomena to Any Future Metaphysics That Will Be Able to Come Forward as Science*, trans. and ed. Gary Hatfield (Cambridge: Cambridge University Press, 2004), 10.
5. Immanuel Kant, *Critique of Pure Reason*, trans. and ed. Paul Guyer and Allen W. Wood (Cambridge: Cambridge University Press, 1997), A760/B788. In the *Lectures on the History of Philosophy*, Hegel writes of the induction argument: 'This is an important and acute observation in relation to experience looked at as the source of knowledge; and it is from this point that the Kantian reflection now begins' (G. W. F. Hegel, *Hegel's Lectures on the History of Philosophy, Volume 3: Medieval and Modern Philosophy*, trans. E. S. Haldane and Frances H. Simson (Lincoln: University of Nebraska Press, 1995), p. 374). He nonetheless prefaces his brief discussion of Hume with the claim that 'the Scepticism of Hume [. . .] has been given a more important place in history than it deserves from its intrinsic nature' (p. 369). Yet another point on which Deleuze and Hegel part ways, which makes the dedication of *Empiricism and Subjectivity* to the great French Hegelian Jean Hyppolite even more striking. On this point, see François Dosse, *Gilles Deleuze and Félix Guattari: Intersecting Lives*, trans. Deborah Glassman (New York: Columbia University Press, 2010), 111.
6. Kant, *Critique of Pure Reason*, B19–20.
7. Kant, *Prolegomena*, 65.
8. In his excellent little essay, 'A Prussian Hume and a Scottish Kant', in *Essays on Kant and Hume* (New Haven, CT: Yale University Press, 1978), 118, Lewis White Beck devotes an important footnote to this 'recollection' (*Erinnerung*).
9. David Hume, Letter 509, in *The Letters of David Hume*, vol. 2, ed. John Young Thomas Greig (Oxford: Clarendon Press, 1983), 301.

10. Quoted in James Feiser, 'Beattie's Lost Letter to the *London Review*', *Hume Studies* 20:1 (1994), 78. Hume is referring to the small-format version of Beattie's book that he must have consulted, i.e. 'it's a small book to contain such a huge lie'.

11. Quentin Meillassoux, *After Finitude*, trans. Ray Brassier (London: Continuum, 2008), 85.

12. For Hume's justly famous breakdown of experience in terms of impressions and ideas, see T 1.1.1. We will return to this in the next chapter.

13. The phrase 'the sun will rise tomorrow' is indeed used by Hume in the *Enquiry*, but only in a footnote devoted to Locke appended to the heading of section 6, 'Of Probability' (EHU 6n9).

14. For an introduction to the place of these principles in Hume's system, and one that emphasises the same productive relationship between critique and construction that powers *Empiricism and Subjectivity*, see John Biro, 'Hume's New Science of the Mind', in *The Cambridge Companion to Hume*, ed. David Fate Norton (Cambridge: Cambridge University Press, 1993), 33–63.

2

Belief and Theoretical Reason

Deleuze emphasises that, for Hume, subjectivity does not and cannot explain experience. It is rather that experience in some way constitutes the subject. It is worth starting our explication of *Empiricism and Subjectivity* properly speaking by asking what precisely is prior to the advent of the subject, and also what precise meaning is to be given to this priority.

What comes before the subject? Once we have abandoned – along with '[a]ll serious writers' (ES 10/27), Deleuze tells us – the conviction that the human mind is a fixed thing, possessing a native structure and its own proper agency, two alternatives appear to be open. The first is to claim that materiality, above all the material machinery of the human animal, precedes subjectivity, 'in which case psychology makes room for physiology' (ES 10/28). This path, taken for instance by neuroscience, consists in the assertion that a certain arrangement of matter is what is prior to and necessary for the advent of human subjectivity.

This path is closed to Hume. The new science of humanity that he proposes has as its single body of evidence our impressions – that is, our atomic perceptions whose source cannot be known – and the ideas that follow from them. The capacity to invoke material bodies as they are in themselves is therefore

19

ruled out. The second path that lies open to Hume is found in precisely this absolute character of impressions, and the ideas that arise from them.

Deleuze writes that, rather than invoking physiology, we can instead propose

> particular principles, constituting a psychic equivalent of matter, wherein psychology finds its conditions, and its only possible object. Hume, with his principles of association, has chosen [this] latter route, which is the most difficult and the most audacious. This is where his sympathy for materialism comes from, and at the same time his reticence toward it. (ES 10/28)

Hume's philosophy – and therefore his account of the advent of the subject – is a philosophy of principles, and it is these that constitute the mind as mind, a thesis we have already briefly discussed. But this does not help us with the primary difficulty. At best it allows us to refine our question, which now becomes: on what material, prior to the mind, do the principles go to work?

The answer is, as we have just said, the ideas that are produced in the mind as copies of impressions. But to put the matter this way is to sell Hume short, according to Deleuze. We cannot avoid invoking impressions here, since they truly are the sole primary content of the mind – they are the mind's *origin* – but it is far more important to register the fact that the ideas that impressions give rise to in the mind are in the first instance *unqualified*: 'There is no constancy or uniformity in the ideas that I have. No more is there constancy or uniformity in the way *in which ideas are connected*' (ES 4/23).

Hume calls this state of the mind *the fancy*. This term derives from the Greek *phantasia*, which names the capacity or power to imagine, that is, to produce images. These images are nothing but the ideas themselves. But since the fancy is purely a capacity for their *production*, ideas are natively disorganised. Invoking Hume's reference to fantastical literature (T 1.1.3.4), Deleuze writes that

Being the place of ideas, the fancy is the collection of separate, individual items. Being the bond of ideas, it moves through the universe, engendering fire dragons, winged horses, and monstrous giants. The depth of the mind is indeed delirium or – the same thing from another point of view – change and indifference. (ES 4/23)

What comes before the subject then is just the collection of ideas in the mind, in their indifferent multiplicity. Now, we must take care, Deleuze writes, with the preposition '*in* the mind'. It would be a mistake to think that the two are separable, and in particular separable into 'thoughts' and 'thinker'. The ideas that form the contents of the mind are the mind itself; the preposition only 'means to ensure the identity of the mind and the ideas of the mind' (ES 3/23).

THE PRINCIPLES OF ASSOCIATION

We have already noted the fact that the principles of human nature, which constitute the means by which the fancy is transformed into an organised structure, cannot themselves be grasped for Hume. We can think them only on the basis of their effects: 'The cause cannot be *known*; principles have neither a cause nor an origin of their power. What is original is their effect upon the imagination' (ES 6/25). But more important again is the fact that the principles themselves, as the capacity to organise the mind, cannot be identified with human nature itself. This was already Deleuze's point in emphasising the identity of the mind and its contents: 'the imagination is not a factor, an agent, or a determining determination' (ES 3/23).

Passing through these negative claims about the principles, we arrive at the key positive assertion. Indeed, 'The most important point is to be found here. The entire sense of the principles of human nature is to transform the *multiplicity* of ideas which constitute the mind into a *system*' (ES 82/80). In the previous chapter, we noted in a preliminary fashion the complexity of this system. Human nature has two complementary, if unequal, facets: 'we are faced, on the one hand, with the effects of association, and on the other with the effects of passion' (ES 16/32). In this chapter, we are interested only in the first of these, its nature, but also its limitations.

Before we say what these principles are, we must note their primary effect: they establish the capacity to form reflectively examined, and therefore justified, *beliefs*. For the fact is that we do possess beliefs about the world, beliefs which are able to be tested and weighed in the light of experience.

Why not talk of knowledge, which has often, since Plato, been defined as true justified belief? The answer is already clear. Since we have literally no way to discover the origin of the impressions we gain through sensation – an impression 'arises in the soul originally, from unknown causes' (T 1.1.2.1), Hume tells us – there exists no independent criterion for establishing truth and falsity. The abyssal character of the fancy is quite stark here, since all belief somehow must be built from the sea of indifferent and chaotically organised ideas that arise from the impressions.

Deleuze and Hume will both use the term 'knowledge' as a name for belief, but to avoid confusion of the two, we will here throughout simply talk of belief.

We have already seen that, for Deleuze, this is not a negative feature of Hume's philosophy but one source of its novelty and force. It is not that we *lack* knowledge, but that knowledge itself must be reconceived such that truth is no longer one of its pertinent criteria. Hume certainly identifies himself as a sceptical philosopher, but here we find the specifically Humean meaning of the term. Unlike, 'ancient skepticism, founded on the variety of sensory appearances and the errors of the senses',[1] whose goal is to insinuate a negative epistemological concern, Hume's modern scepticism is aligned with the positive project of justifying belief, of the judicious examination and determination of the likelihood of our beliefs. In fact, in the following brilliant passage of the *Treatise*, Hume insists that this is *all* we are capable of doing:

Should it here be asked me, whether I sincerely assent to this argument [for absolute doubt], which I seem to take such pains to inculcate, and whether I be really one of those sceptics, who hold that all is uncertain, and that our judgment is not in any thing possest of any measures of truth and falshood; I should reply, that *this question is entirely superfluous*, and that neither I, nor any other person was ever sincerely and constantly of that opinion. Nature, by an absolute and uncontroulable necessity has determined us to judge as well as to breathe and feel; nor can we any more forbear viewing certain objects in a stronger and fuller light, upon account of their customary connexion with a present impression, than we can hinder ourselves from thinking as long, as we are awake, or seeing the surrounding bodies, when we turn our eyes towards them in broad sunshine. Whoever has taken the pains to refute the cavils of this total scepticism, has really disputed without an antagonist, and endeavoured by arguments to establish a faculty, which nature has antecedently implanted in the mind, and *rendered unavoidable*. (T 1.4.1.7; emphases added)

Beliefs exist in the mind – but where do they come from? The answer brings us to the principles of association themselves. The following text will guide us here:

Constancy and uniformity are present only in the way *in which ideas are associated in the imagination*. Association with its three principles (contiguity, resemblance, and causality), transcends the imagination, and also differs from it. Association affects the imagination [. . .] It is a quality which unifies ideas, not a quality of ideas themselves. (ES 4/23–4)

We will return to this use of the term 'imagination' shortly, which for the moment can be taken as a synonym for the mind itself (just as Deleuze does (ES 4/22)). However, all of the ingredients to understand the basic function of association are here.

Hume identifies three distinct principles of association. The first is contiguity in time and space. Here, one idea may be habitually associated with another if their corresponding impressions arose in temporal proximity – the cigars I smoked

23

that summer with her are associated in my mind, and now each time I smoke a cigar, the idea of her returns. But the same holds for the ideas I have of cigars and the vintage lighter which used to lie next to each other on the table by the bed.

Resemblance, the second principle, is as easy to grasp. I tend to associate ideas that in some way resemble one another. This is how, for instance, if you have never smoked a cigar, it remains possible to form ideas of the summer fling and the melancholic association of the cigar invoked above, just as it is possible to form a belief about what someone actually looks like in person by looking at a picture of them.

Cause and effect, finally, is the tendency to associate ideas in terms of the causal relation. We associate the white ball's motion and collision with the movement of the red ball, but equally we infer the existence of parents from the fact of our friend's existence. The fact that the causal association runs – neutrally, without essential orientation – in both directions will take on particular importance later. We must also insist on the singularity of cause and effect in comparison with the other two principles of association, a point Deleuze stresses throughout *Empiricism and Subjectivity*: 'we must make a special place for causality' (ES 131/115). The great power of the causal association is that it alone of the principles of association necessarily involves an inference (*if this then that*). This is, equally, its threat to legitimate beliefs, since in doing so it invites us to overstep the boundaries of experience and make direct claims about reality. We will return to this point shortly.

In turn, the principles of association have three kinds of general or schematic (ES 144/127) effects, or produce three general kinds of beliefs. Deleuze summarises them as follows:

> Sometimes the idea takes on a role and becomes capable of representing all these ideas with which, through resemblance, it is associated (general idea); at other times, the union of ideas brought about *by* the mind acquires a regularity not previously had, in which case 'nature in a manner point[s] out to every one those

simple ideas, which are most proper to be united into a complex one' (substance and mode); finally, sometimes, one idea can introduce another (relation). (ES 6/25, quoting T 1.1.4.1)

For instance, a resemblance between a large number of things might lead us to treat them as cases of one general type of thing (from particular urban environments to the idea of the city). In the case of substance–mode relations, at issue is the association of particular ideas into a unified thing and its accidental properties (the apple, which is now green but may later be red).

These three kinds of effects are not themselves beliefs, even though we can, in examining the beliefs we have, see that they all in one way or another fall into these categories. What precisely is belief then? It is not the principles themselves of course, but neither is it their immediate effect. Association produces in the mind not beliefs but *habitual tendencies*. 'The result of association', Deleuze writes, gives rise to 'the mind's easy passage from one idea to another, so that the essence of relations becomes precisely this easy transition. The mind, having become nature, has acquired now a *tendency*' (ES 7/25). Already, then, we see how we might pass from the indifferent chaos of the fancy to a structured order in the mind. As Deleuze puts it near the end of *Empiricism and Subjectivity*, using a fluid-mechanical metaphor,

> The principles of association establish natural relations among ideas, forming inside the mind an entire network similar to a system of channels. No longer do we move accidentally from one idea to another. One idea naturally introduces another on the basis of a principle; ideas naturally follow one another. (ES 139/123)

In turn, beliefs are the products of these associative tendencies. A belief that the white ball caused the red ball to move on the billiard table is the result of a certain habit to associate particular ideas rather than others. Presenting examples like this, piecemeal, of course overlooks the fact that the belief about causation involved in playing billiards is intertwined with innumerable others. Nevertheless, it is indeed true that 'the effects of the principles of association are complex ideas' (ES 112/101).

Beliefs, therefore, are the ultimate products of the principles of association. They constitute claims about the world that the world itself – which is only available to us in the form of the impressions garnered by sensation – does not license. For this reason, the term that Deleuze will finally alight on to describe beliefs is 'transcendence' (*transcendance*).[2] 'It is transcendence or going beyond. I affirm more than I know' (ES 11/28). Particular beliefs about cause and effect relations, for instance, transcend what is given *to* experience, because cause and effect relations are not given *in* experience. Thus, 'in the case of causality the relation is *transcendence*' (ES 111/100).

The term 'transcendence' is not one often associated with Deleuze's philosophy, and in fact famous texts throughout his work attack it in the name of the univocity of being, and the thesis of immanence. However, what these latter texts concern themselves with is the ontological sense we might give to the term, as if there existed a hierarchy in being between two fixed and established orders – such as we find in the Cartesian division of mind and body. In Hume, as Deleuze reads him, no such claim is at issue, and nor could it be. Being is never what is at stake in Hume, since the entirety of our encounter with being is located at the limits of the mind, and its origin can only be traced back to the original fact of sensible impressions. To believe is to go beyond the given, a claim that only pertains to the structural ordering of ideas in the mind. And, in this sense and quite simply, 'Transcendence is an empirical fact' (ES 125/111).

THE ORIGIN AND NATURE OF ILLEGITIMATE BELIEFS

It is of the highest importance that the object of the principles of association is properly understood. They are rules for the organisation of *ideas*, and nothing else. We must always keep in mind the fact that Hume's sceptical take-down of claims about objective causal relations and the insistence on the value and necessity of causality as a principle are perfectly compatible, even reciprocally required theses. The fact that I believe the movement of the red ball was caused when the white ball hit it can be explained not with reference to some kind of intellectual intuition of objective causality, but by the habitual association of ideas in the mind.

However, it is here that a new problem arises for belief. The principles of association give rise to habitual connections in the mind, but these connections are, strictly speaking, ungrounded. That I happen to associate the cigar and the bedside table is absolutely contingent, but so too is the association between the white and the red ball, or between a spider bite and poisoning. The fact is that no guardrail exists that could prevent association from habituating entirely false beliefs.

Take the cause and effect association. I may conclude from experience that my blue shirt is lucky. Each time I wear it, the lecture goes well, or I write particularly well, or I manage to avoid catastrophe at dinner. I infer that the shirt is the cause of these happy effects in my life, but this inference, though it arises in the same way as the belief that water always boils at 100°C, is illegitimate. 'By itself, habit can feign or invoke a false experience, and bring about belief through "a repetition" which "is not deriv'd from experience." This will be an illegitimate belief' (ES 66/69, quoting T 1.3.9.8). Or consider racism, which would presuppose the formation of a belief that all people who resemble each other in a certain way possess certain necessary characteristics (formation of a fictional general idea).

From the point of view of the principles of association, there is nothing to say of these cases than that beliefs are created. The source of illegitimate beliefs – beliefs that are unjustified in the light of experience – is therefore nothing other than the source of legitimate beliefs. In a short text that summarises the main arguments of *Empiricism and Subjectivity* published in 1972, Deleuze puts the matter this way:

> if it is true that the principles of association determine the mind by imposing on it a nature to discipline its delirium or fictions of the imagination, conversely the imagination uses these same principles

to pass off its fictions and fantasies as real, lending them a surety they would not otherwise have. In this sense, what is proper to fiction is feigning the relations themselves.[3]

Deleuze makes use of religion, one of Hume's major objects of critical engagement, to illustrate this problem. The plausibility of monotheism is in part found in the fact that the natural world appears to us to possess a unity and purpose. Theistic belief is also supported by the experience of the exceptional or its reports – miracles – but also by the more mundane repetitions that belong to ritual. At the more intellectual level, we find the arguments for God's existence. The argument from analogy, for instance, tells us that God must exist qua creator, since finite mechanisms like watches, themselves already complicated, require a creator, and the world is infinitely more complex than a watch. Another argument, known as the teleological argument, tells us that the chain of causes that we witness in the natural world must have had a first cause at the origin of the sequence: God.

These five points are all cases in which the principles of association are deployed in an illegitimate fashion not justified by experience. The apparent unity and purpose of the natural world are only the products of the principles of the association – the natural world is 'the sort of unity which only resemblance and causality can guarantee in phenomenon' (ES 72/73) – and cannot be legitimately attributed to the world itself. Liturgical ritual ensconces belief through the mechanism of habit itself (repetition of similar cases), but in doing so relies upon this mechanism to function without the need to justify what is being said. Here, spoken repetition and empirical evidence change places, and the latter comes to be judged on the grounds of the former. Conversely, in the famous case of miracles, an exception to the natural order is held up as evidence of a purposeful divine order. But as Hume argues in his famous text on this topic, the natural world, being produced entirely through the principles of association, can brook no exceptions. Hence Hume's famous claim in the first *Enquiry* that 'A miracle is a violation of the laws of nature; and as a firm and unalterable experience has established these laws, the proof against a miracle, from the very nature of the fact, is as entire as any argument from experience can possibly be imagined' (EHU 10.12).

As for the arguments from analogy and causality, both also exceed what is given to us in experience. In the case of analogy, there is in fact very little in common between the natural world and a watch, unless we prejudicially select only those features that are salient to the argument. Resemblance is deployed selectively such that it increases the plausibility of the argument by downplaying the differences that might trouble it. The teleological argument is an even more obvious case, since it baldly deploys the causal association beyond what, by definition, we could ever directly encounter.

Now, the very problem here is that, however suspect theism might appear, it is produced in precisely the same fashion as legitimate beliefs. At the limit, 'To believe in miracles is a false belief, but it is also a true miracle' (ES 77/76). In sum, if we stay at this level of the application of the principles, it seems that we really have not escaped the mad indifference of the fancy after all, or rather, 'the mind is still fancy on another level and in a new way' (ES 53/59). It has been granted new powers, and access to a new regime in which it can extend its effects. The fancy

> finds here an entirely new extension. The fancy can always invoke relations, borrow the clothing of nature, and form general rules, going beyond the determined field of legitimate knowledge and carrying knowledge beyond its proper limits. (ES 7/25)

Because all belief transcends the given, all belief is at once well founded, absolutely suspect and apparently unimpeachable.

THEORETICAL REASON

Later in the book, we will return to the phenomenon of illegitimate belief in more detail. For now, we can simply observe that Hume's account does not leave us in this abyssal situation.

Deleuze designates the primary application of the principles of association as *extensive*. They allow us to transcend the given, that is, the ensemble of ideas in the mind: we believe. But, as we have just seen, we believe too much; habit sanctifies too many things. We are 'only able to believe by falsifying belief in the confusion of the accidental and the general' (ES 69/71).

The extensive use of the principles must therefore be doubled with a *corrective* use. It is only this twofold deployment of rules for belief that can correct for the errancy proper to association. The goal of this corrective application will be to limit the formation of beliefs to only what can be vouched for by the ideas that I possess, that is, ideas that arose on the basis of past impressions. In turn, 'This task is accomplished to the extent that the act of belief bears exclusively upon an object being determined in accordance with [. . .] repetitions observed in experience' (ES 71/72).

Belief would thus continue to transcend the given, while remaining bound within its sphere. How is this to be accomplished? How can the accidental and the general be rightfully distinguished? The ultimate difference between legitimate and illegitimate beliefs, as we know, is that the latter are not supported by experience. The blue shirt seems to bring me luck – and in this it shares the logic of the argument from analogy for God's existence – only because a very small set of experiences is selected to support this belief. If I was to broaden this set to include more situations in which I was wearing the shirt, I would increasingly begin to see that my former belief was unfounded.

The means deployed here is straightforwardly that of '*comparison*' (ES 65). At issue is the comparison of a particular current belief with the suite of my previous beliefs. The fact is that we never form any belief once and for all. All beliefs are involved in a constant process of reinforcement and contestation, due to the fact that each new experience will have to be accounted for through the process of association. When I am presented with an idea that troubles the belief that I currently hold, it becomes a matter of weighing up the likelihood of its correctness in light of the other beliefs that I hold.

> Undoubtedly, the characteristic of belief, inference and reasoning is to transcend experience and to transfer the past to the future; but it is still necessary that the object of belief be determined in accordance with a past experience. (ES 70/71)

Now, because no belief is absolute – no belief characterises knowledge in the strong sense – there is no question of ruling out any belief absolutely. The current belief can only be weighed in terms of its likelihood against the backdrop of the beliefs previously obtained. The corrective mechanism is therefore essentially a calculus of probabilities.

This corrective deployment of habit Deleuze will designate as *experimental* or *theoretical reason*, and its product is what Hume calls philosophical probability. It is to be distinguished from nonphilosophical probability – like that found in the assertion that my shirt is lucky, or 'Irishmen cannot have wit' (ES 67/69; T 1.3.13.7) – which is found in all beliefs that result from the primary extensive deployment of the principles, and thus come to the same thing as the set of uncorrected beliefs themselves. In turn, the central aim of theoretical reason is to produce a body of beliefs that have been tested against the tapestry of the beliefs that came before.

Reason here must not be taken to be anything like the Cartesian or Spinozist *ratio*. Leaving aside the fact that reason for Hume is 'a calm determination of the passions' (T 3.3.1.17), 'is a kind of feeling' (ES 14/30) – a fact that we will return to later – it is not independent of habitual association and experience. 'In fact, experimental reason is born of habit – and not vice versa. Habit is the root of reason, and indeed the principle from which reason stems as an effect' (ES 62/66). If we engage in this kind of corrective application of habit, it is because this is itself a habit, in addition to the tripartite habit of association.

THE INSUFFICIENCY OF CORRECTIVE RULES FOR BELIEF

But now we come to a third act in the drama of belief. Unlike the classical third act in the theatre or narrative cinema, however, it brings us to a troubling realisation rather than an encompassing resolution.

We can see what this is by pursuing the example of theism a little further. Theism turns around a belief in the extra-sensory existence of a divine being. The belief in God may be produced through any or all of the mechanisms we saw earlier, and, like any belief, it may be corrected to a certain extent. Deleuze will even suggest that, in Hume, religious belief tends towards being corrected out of existence (ES 76/76). But the terminus of this correction can never be attained. This is due to the nature of the belief in God itself. On the one hand, it is produced on the basis of repetitions that are not repetitions of direct experiences of God – they come from social practices like liturgy – so the belief itself cannot be rationally adjusted. On the other, while we can never produce direct positive evidence of the existence of God in experience, 'we can always think of God negatively, as the cause of the principles' (ES 77/77).

Deleuze continues, noting that 'It is in this sense that theism is valid' (ES 77/77), but it would be better to say that it possesses a peculiar paravalidity. The problem clearly appears here. We are capable of producing beliefs that cannot be positively corrected for, a correlate of the fact that all such corrections proceed on the basis of probability rather than certainty. And again, beliefs like the belief in God, rather than being somehow exceptional in their excessiveness, are paradigmatic, appearing as 'the horizon of every possible belief, or as the lowest degree of belief. Because if everything is belief, everything is a question of the degrees of belief, even the delirium of non-understanding.'[4]

In short, we are never completely justified in discarding those beliefs that cannot be subordinated to the calculus of probability, because the latter is our sole means for such a justification. This is the conceptual context in which Deleuze would place the brilliant and very famous closing passages of the first book of the *Treatise*, a text that every book on Hume should cite:

> Methinks I am like a man, who having struck on many shoals, and having narrowly escaped shipwreck in passing a small frith, has yet the temerity to put out to sea in the same leaky weather-beaten vessel, and even carries his ambition so far as to think of compassing the globe under these disadvantageous circumstances. My memory of past errors and perplexities, makes me diffident for the future. The wretched condition, weakness, and disorder of the faculties, I must employ in my enquiries, encrease my apprehensions. And the impossibility of amending or correcting these faculties, reduces me almost to despair, and makes me resolve to perish on the barren rock, on which I am at present, rather than venture myself upon that boundless ocean, which runs out into immensity. This sudden view of my danger strikes me with melancholy; and as it is usual for that passion, above all others, to indulge itself; I cannot forbear feeding my despair, with all those desponding reflections, which the present subject furnishes me with in such abundance. (T 1.4.12.1)

In Chapter 4, we will discuss in more detail the range of uncorrectable beliefs Deleuze invokes, and the kind of situation that the believing subject is put in by the role played by belief in subjectivity. But what must be added is that the system of the understanding – the system of beliefs engendered through habitual association and their correction through reason – does not exhaust subjectivity. Indeed, its decisive moral, social and political facet remains to be investigated. And it is this that will provide us with the means to bridge the chasm in rational reflection that Hume exposes. Indeed, this is already very clear in the case of theism, since the belief in God and its consequences are modulated and circumscribed by social institutions (or alternatively, allowed to flourish or encouraged to grotesquely inflate) there where the understanding and reason find themselves entirely powerless. But the solution is already to be found *in nuce* in the means by which the Humean resolves their melancholy:

> Where am I, or what? From what causes do I derive my existence, and to what condition shall I return? Whose favour shall I court, and whose anger must I dread? What beings surround me? and on whom have, I any influence, or who have any influence on me? I am confounded with all these questions, and begin to fancy myself in the most deplorable condition imaginable, invironed with the deepest darkness, and utterly deprived of the use of every member and faculty.
>
> Most fortunately it happens, that since reason is incapable of dispelling these clouds, nature herself suffices to that purpose, and cures me of this philosophical melancholy and delirium, either by relaxing this bent of mind, or by some avocation, and lively impression of my senses, which obliterate all these chimeras. I dine, I play a game of backgammon, I converse, and am merry with my friends; and when after three or four hours' amusement, I would return to these speculations, they appear so cold, and strained, and ridiculous, that I cannot find in my heart to enter into them any farther. (T 1.4.12.8–9)

THE IMAGINATION AND THE SUBSISTENT STRUCTURE OF THE MIND

We must make two final, interrelated points before considering the place of the passions, morality and society in *Empiricism and Subjectivity*. In this chapter, we have passed from the fancy to the understanding and reason by way of the principles of association, as if outlining three successive moments in a developmental process. But such an account can be misleading.

This is due, in the first instance, to the apparently temporal sequence involved. At the start of the chapter, I remarked that the question 'what is prior to the subject?' requires us to ask what exactly 'prior' means. Indeed, it cannot be temporal in nature, even though it is clearly true that the process of habit formation is gradual (ES 61/65). But this gradual process is the correlate of a structural coexistence. The disorganised state of the mind is not somehow consumed in the formation of habitual structures, but rather subsists, providing the relational structure of the mind (associationism) with the material to which it is applied (atomism). This is why Deleuze will write that 'The paradox of habit is that it is at once formed by degrees and a principle of human nature' (ES 62/66).

Deleuze's use of the phrase 'depth [*fond*] of the mind' (ES 4/23) when characterising the fancy is key here, and finds parallels in two of his often-cited sources, Leibniz and Freud. Something akin to the cacophony of Leibniz's *petits perceptions* is in play – beneath the unified representation of a single wave crashing on the beach are the innumerable infinitely small perceptions of the droplets of water, and the droplets within those. Or again, there is here a certain idea of the unconscious, the unregulated play of images that have arisen from sensory encounters and are, in themselves, organised according to indifferent chance.

We must also insist on the fact that, for Deleuze, Hume's philosophy is from start to finish a philosophy of the imagination. Neither belief, nor understanding, nor reason are native faculties in the mind; all that belongs to it naturally and by right is the capacity to *spontaneously produce images*. It is this that unifies and underwrites the various emergent faculties of the mind, or rather, to be more precise, is all of these faculties, variously modulated. Thus, the fancy is nothing other than the imagination grasped in its own state, as if unaffected by the principles: 'By itself, the imagination is not nature; it is a mere fancy' (ES 4/23), and 'Hume constantly affirms the identity between the mind, the imagination, and ideas' (ES 3/22). But it is equally the support for all belief, legitimate and illegitimate, the locus of critical reason, and more: 'memory, the senses, and understanding are [. . .] all of them founded on the imagination, or the vivacity of our ideas' (T 1.4.7.3). Indeed, we can even define the resemblance, contiguity and causality solely in its terms: 'The role of the principles of association is to fix the imagination' (ES 60/65).

Morality too, as we will now see, falls under the general heading of 'imagination', insofar as it concerns the production of general rules. We will in fact come to see why it is that 'the illusion of the fancy is the reality of culture' (ES 57/62).

NOTES

1. Gilles Deleuze, 'Hume', in *Desert Islands and Other Texts*, ed. David Lapoujade, trans. Michael Taormina (New York: Semiotext(e), 2004), 166.
2. It is worth noting that, for the most part, Deleuze uses *dépassement* rather than *transcendance*. Boundas is nonetheless correct, in my view, to translate the former as 'transcendence'. Deleuze himself explicitly treats the terms as equivalents at one point in *Empiricism and Subjectivity*: '*Dans la connaissance, quel est le fait? La transcendance ou le dépassement: j'affirme plus que je ne sais, mon jugement dépasse l'idée*' (ES 11/28). Deleuze will moreover link the two terms together very clearly in the context of a survey of the theme of transcendence itself in a 1956 lecture series – in which Hume figures in the very terms we are invoking here – entitled 'What is Grounding?' (Gilles Deleuze, *What is Grounding?*, trans. Arjen Kleinherenbrink, ed. Tony Yanick, Jason Adams and Mohammad Salemy (Grand Rapids: &&& Publishing, 2015), 24–7).
3. Deleuze, 'Hume', 165.
4. Deleuze, 'Hume', 166.

3

The Moral World

The means by which beliefs are engendered in the mind appear to leave it freewheeling in the indifferent abyss of the fancy. Without firm foundations, we are as liable to endorse the most outrageously fictitious assertion as a well-justified belief. It is of the greatest importance to stress the fundamental nature of this problem, which concerns not the local perturbations of experience around a game of billiards, but the most general and consequential of beliefs concerning God, the self and the world.

But we have just begun to lay out Deleuze's reconstruction of Hume. Moreover, we have already briefly seen the resolution that it will present to the madness of the fancy: society. Nobody plays backgammon alone, of course, but more broadly it is the way in which the inner life of the mind is rooted in the social order which orients belief and theoretical reason, and gives them their *raison d'être*.

The explanation of this claim will also lead to a resolution of a different problem, namely the incapacity of reason to motivate subjective action. The fact that certain ideas are associated in the mind provides us with no reason to do anything, and reason possesses no motivational force whatsoever. This is why Deleuze asserts, as I have already noted, that the 'principal sentence of the *Treatise* is this: "'Tis not contrary to reason to prefer the destruction of the whole world to the scratching of my finger"' (ES 18/33, quoting T 2.3.3.6). Another famous claim of Hume's makes the same point: 'Reason is, and ought only to be the slave of the passions and can never pretend to any other office than to serve and obey them' (T 2.3.3.4). The recourse to intersubjectivity – to morality and politics – that this chapter will outline thus functions at once as the ultimate *corrective* to the excesses of the fancy, and the *motivation* for practical activity in accordance with, if beyond, the system of the understanding.

Before we continue our elaboration of Deleuze's Hume, a couple of notes. The first concerns an issue of translation. Deleuze's mature philosophy, under the principal influences of Nietzsche and Spinoza, will direct a relentless critique at the notion of morality, counterposing to it the notion of an ethics of capacity. The question of what to do will no longer be posed in terms of what I *ought* to do, but what I am *capable* of doing. For this reason, no doubt, Constantin Boundas quite often translates *la morale* and *la moralité* as 'ethics'. In Hume's own work, however, and in *Empiricism and Subjectivity* as a result, the latter term only appears very infrequently indeed (four times in the *Treatise* by my count, compared with nearly two hundred uses of moral and its cognates). The choice may not seem particularly significant, leading at most to a minor confusion for readers of Hume unfamiliar with Deleuze. But what must be insisted upon – and why the choice of 'moral' is faithful to both the letter and spirit of Hume's philosophy – is that for Hume morality certainly is concerned with *ought*. It is true that, on Deleuze's reading, this ought is the subject of a social and political genesis that arises on non-normative grounds, but to pose Hume as a non-moral thinker is to threaten to confuse the general goal of his investigation into society, politics and, yes, morality. For this reason, Boundas's choice is unfortunate, akin to translating the title of Nietzsche's masterpiece as *The Genealogy of Ethics*.[1]

Equally puzzling, though, are some of the terminological choices made by Deleuze himself. In seeking to draw a parallel between the formation of the system of the understanding and the system of morality, Deleuze will speak of the principles of the passions – a phrase which, as I have already noted, Hume himself does not use. Deleuze's most common claim in this conjunction is that the passions themselves function as analogues of the principles of association: 'the principles of morality, that is, the original and natural qualities of the passions, transcend and affect the mind, just as the principles of association do' (ES 19/34). But at times he draws a much more straightforward parallel, saying for instance that the principles of the passions can be presented under 'the general form of the principle of utility' (ES 109/98), referring us to Hume's analysis of promising (see T 3.2.5). But to see what this way of framing the matter amounts to, we first need to understand what Hume means by the passions themselves.

FROM THE PASSIONS TO MORALITY

Deleuze's account of morality in Hume moves very quickly onto the terrain of the famous Humean concept of sympathy, and in doing so spends little time discussing the nature of the passions themselves. Because his account nevertheless presupposes certain elements of this discussion, it will be worth briefly outlining them here.

Like his attack on dogmatic claims about the nature of knowledge, Hume's account of morality begins by returning us to the elementary situation of sensory experience. Somewhat optimistically – above all given his analysis of the fact that human nature is always prey to erroneous beliefs – Hume will frame his account in the *Enquiry concerning the Principles of Morality* in the following way:

> Men are now cured of their passion for hypotheses and systems in natural philosophy, and will hearken to no arguments but those which are derived from experience. It is full time they should attempt a like reformation in all moral disquisitions; and reject every system of ethics, however subtle or ingenious, which is not founded on fact and observation. (EPM 1.1.9)

What do we discover at the root of morality when we attend only to the facts? Unsurprisingly, *impressions* – and specifically the impressions of pleasure and pain. But, once again as in the case of belief, these impressions themselves do not explain anything. While it is very important that moral values are ultimately grounded in affects rather than reason, what really matters are the consequences that arise in the mind from them, namely the passions themselves.

The term designates everything that we would normally describe as emotions – one of Hume's lists, for example, includes 'pride, humility, ambition, vanity, love, hatred, envy, pity, malice, generosity, [. . .] desire, aversion, grief, joy, hope, fear, despair and security' (T 2.1.1.3). Some of these terms are no longer used in the same way – for example, what Hume means by humility is closer to what we mean by shame – but it is easy to see in general outline that he aims to include the full range of human emotions in his account of the passions.

Hume's goal is to explain how moral values arise from the impressions of pain and pleasure, and in this regard it is a near analogue of the problematic of belief examined in the previous chapter. Unlike this case, though, in which a wide variety of complex effects arise in the same way (habitual association), there are two distinct kinds of effects that arise in the mind in the wake of pleasure and pain. Hume distinguishes between *direct* and *indirect* passions.[2] Direct passions are immediate consequences of pleasure or pain, or any experience that seems to promise them. Indirect passions, on the other hand, require the presence of an idea that will be the object of the passion. In the case of pride, for instance, the idea of the self is joined to the impression of pleasure; in malice, it is the idea of another person's suffering that is joined to the impression.

As Deleuze puts it, 'indirect passions proceed from good and evil, "but by the conjunction with other qualities": a relation of an idea must be added to the relation of impressions' (ES 134/117–18, quoting T 2.1.1.3). Implicit here is the notion that the indirect passions require in some way the principles of association, a point we will return to shortly.

Hume is careful to emphasise that the *object* of an indirect passion must not be confused with its *cause*. In a discussion of love and hate (pleasure and pain involving another person as their object), he presents the following argument on this point:

> though the object of love and hatred be always some other person, it is plain that the object is not, properly speaking, the cause of these passions, or alone sufficient to excite them. For since love and hatred are directly contrary in their sensation, and have the same object in common, if that object were also their cause, it would produce these opposite passions in an equal degree; and as they must, from the very first moment, destroy each other, none of them would ever be able to make its appearance. There must, therefore, be some cause different from the object. (T 2.2.1.3)

The cause of all passions is always finally impressions of pleasure and pain, and the difference between direct and indirect passions only turns around the particular mechanism that unfolds their consequences.

Let us observe a crucial point by way of consequence: the passions are themselves neither impressions of sensation, since they do not arise directly in response to the world, nor are they ideas, since they are not copies of such impressions. They are in fact a second-order impression, or what Hume calls *impressions of reflection*: 'This idea of pleasure or pain, when it returns upon the soul, produces the new impressions of desire and aversion, hope and fear, which may properly be called impressions of reflexion, because derived from it' (T 1.1.2.1). This distinction between two kinds of impressions is arguably the key element in Deleuze's reconstruction of Hume, and we shall have a lot to say about it when we turn to the topic of subjectivity. For the moment, we should just note that what Deleuze calls the principles of the passions are best conceived as the means by which the passage from one order of impressions to the other is effected. Why do I feel pride in the poem I have just finished?

I experience some pleasure in its completion, and this in turn gives rise to the passion. The principles of association give rise to complex ideas, that is, beliefs; the principles of the passions give rise to impressions of reflection. In both cases, nothing further can be said about the origin of the principles or their power in the mind. We observe the ubiquity and regularity of the principles of human nature's effects, and that is all.

Hume will now add a further distinction between 'the calm and the VIOLENT' (T 2.1.1.3). Passions of the latter kind are easy to conceive – raging anger, a profound longing for someone else, or a lust that obliterates all thought. The former, which Hume will sometimes distinguish by calling them 'emotions', are a much more interesting group, and include things like the appreciation of beauty and composition in art, and – most striking of all – reason itself, a point we shall return to below. Unlike the distinction between direct and indirect passions, though, this is clearly a matter of degrees, such that the same passion can be at one time strong and violent, and another calm. It is even possible for particularly calm passions to 'decay into so soft an emotion, as to become, in a manner, imperceptible' (T 2.1.1.3). In fact, at this end of the spectrum, passions (as impressions of reflection) are very close indeed – and sometimes practically indistinguishable – from ideas.

What, though, gives any of this a *moral* dimension? The question, easy to formulate in response to Hume, is nevertheless a bad (or at least misleading) one. For Hume, moral problems can only be posed in terms of the passions, and these in turn are explicable solely in terms of pleasure and pain. Put another way, what makes the passions a matter of morality does not involve any moral features that naturally belong to them. Morality is a human product that is founded on, rather than being antecedent to or separable from, the affective order.

If we are led to pose such a question, it is perhaps because we suspect that an extra-affective quality – a *rational* quality – belongs to moral decision-making. We know, though, that reason is a function of association and addresses itself solely to ideas, and not impressions. After the opening section of the third book of the *Treatise* – 'Moral Distinctions Not Deriv'd from Reason' – Hume writes:

> Now, since the distinguishing impressions, by which moral good or evil is known, are nothing but particular pains or pleasures; it follows, that in all enquiries concerning these moral distinctions, it will be sufficient to shew the principles, which make us feel a satisfaction or uneasiness from the survey of any character, in order to satisfy us why the character is laudable or blameable. An action, or sentiment, or character is virtuous or vicious; why? because its view causes a pleasure or uneasiness of a particular kind. (T 3.1.2.3)

Later he is even more direct:

> The approbation of moral qualities most certainly is not derived from reason, or any comparison of ideas; but proceeds entirely from a moral taste, and from certain sentiments of pleasure or disgust, which arise upon the contemplation and view of particular qualities or characters. (T 3.3.1.14)

But such a question does conceal an important concern, and it involves the place of other people in moral reasoning. So far, it would appear that the effective solipsism we find in Hume's account of belief has been asserted once again in morality, there where it is least obviously true. But at this point, we finally arrive back at *Empiricism and Subjectivity*, and the first major element of Hume's moral thought that Deleuze will engage with in detail: the category of sympathy.

SYMPATHY

Sympathy is our basic and indisputable concern for the well-being of certain others to whom we are close, members of our families in the first instance. We experience passions for and about ourselves, but we also include others in this concern. It is sympathy that 'makes us abandon, without inference, our own point of view' (ES 23/37). Here is Hume in the *Enquiry concerning the Principles of Morality*:

> It is needless to push our researches so far as to ask, why we have humanity or a fellow-feeling with others. It is sufficient, that this is experienced to be a principle in human nature. [. . .] No man is absolutely indifferent to the happiness and misery of others. The first has a natural tendency to give pleasure; the second, pain. This every one may find in himself. It is not probable, that these principles can be resolved into principles more simple and universal, whatever attempts may have been made to that purpose. (EPM 5.2n1)

So the answer to the question concerning the place of others in the passion play of morality will be resolved in terms of sympathy. How does sympathy function? When I see my brother break into a smile, it tends to make me also smile, and to feel pleasure. I must first, Hume says, infer from my experience of his behaviour the belief he is experiencing the passion of joy for some reason. But this only provides me with an *idea* of my brother's pleasure, and not a passion. The second moment involves a further inference, this time on the basis of our resemblance to one another – not only as brothers, but ultimately as two human beings. He, the one who is smiling, is *like me*. And because – third moment – I know what it is like to be a human being, the idea of my brother's pleasure is infused with a new vivacity, such that I now feel pleasure along with him.

The mechanism of sympathy here is akin to a fuse that, when lit by another's (inferred) passions, burns all the way back into the self and effects a transformation of a relatively neutral idea into a more vivacious impression. The result is the easy passage of the passions from other to self. In this way, joy and sadness, love and hatred, attain a certain independence from particular people, and we begin to be able to treat them in general. The moral judgements that they might give rise to likewise begin to take on a general character. As Deleuze puts it, 'The feeling which prompts us to praise or blame, the pain and pleasure which determine vice and virtue, have an original nature: they are produced with reference to character *in general*' (ES 23/37).

Making use of a helpful musical metaphor – something that Hume himself does at important moments, as we will see later – David Fate Norton puts the point this way:

> Human beings, Hume suggests, resonate among themselves like strings of the same length wound to the same tension. Consequently, when one of us observes a quality or character that has a tendency to the good of other individuals or of humanity itself, and whose operation produces, or may be expected to produce, pleasure in others, we ourselves resonate with the pleasure of those others. We ourselves neither receive nor expect to receive any direct benefit from the observed quality, but our sympathetic link to it causes us to approve it.[3]

But now a problem emerges: sympathy is naturally – and dramatically – limited in scope. An act of kindness performed by my brother give rise to pleasure for me, and my sense, consequently, that the act is a morally good one. At the same time, if an act of kindness is performed on behalf of someone unknown to me by someone equally unknown, but also happens to cause my brother sadness, I will tend to experience pain, not pleasure, will not call the act good or endorse it as kind. Hume writes that

> Whoever is united to us by any connexion is always sure of a share of our love, proportioned to the connexion, without enquiring into his other qualities. Thus the relation of blood produces the strongest tie the mind is capable of in the love of parents to their children, and a lesser degree of the same affection, as the relation lessens. (T 2.2.4.2)[4]

Consequently, it is even the case that 'We condemn the parents who prefer strangers to their own children' (ES 24/38, invoking T 3.2.2.8). A parallel appears at this point between the elementary situations of morality and belief respectively. In the latter case, the only materials we have to work with are *parts*, or atoms, that is, the impressions and their ideas-copies. In morality, at this elementary level of sympathy, we must begin with the fact of our *partiality*. Thus the following 'paradox of sympathy': 'it opens up for us a moral space and a generality, but this space is without extension [*cette étendue même est sans extension*], a generality without quantity' (ES 23/37).

This partiality is the major obstacle to the formation of morality in any meaningful sense. The natural limits of sympathy, along with the plurality of affects, the hope for intersubjective harmony seems snuffed out from the start: 'we are confronted with contradiction and violence' (ES 25/38). But here we must be particularly careful not to subsume this Humean account to one that leads to the same conclusions but for very different reasons: egoism.

The egoist view holds that human beings are selfish, and in the final analysis only ever have their own interests in mind. *Homo homini lupus*: man is wolf to man in this merciless state of human nature. For Hume, such a thesis is an absolute falsity and non-starter, one that runs against the most obvious evidence. Deleuze cites a part of a scathing passage (ES 25/38) that reads more fully:

> Consult common experience: Do you not see, that though the whole expence of the family be generally under the direction of the master of it, yet there are few that do not bestow the largest part of their fortunes on the pleasures of their wives, and the education of their children, reserving the smallest portion for their own proper use and entertainment. (T 3.2.2.5)

The truth is that, contrary to the fictions of the egoist, we are always already a part of a minimal social world, one whose fundamental structure is provided not by irreducible competition but sympathy. On this point, it would be hard for Hume to be any clearer: 'we must renounce the theory, which accounts for every moral sentiment by the principle of self-love' (EPM 5.2.2).

Deleuze further notes that the opposition between sympathy and egoism is also an opposition of two conceptions of society, and that great misunderstandings of both nature and culture arise when we mistake the limited reach of our sympathy for selfishness: 'This is why it is so important to be reminded that the natural human being is not egotistical; our entire notion of society depends on it' (ES 26/39). The egoist viewpoint will, and *can only*, present society as a negative mechanism for the constraint of our alleged selfishness, and consists in imposing juridical restrictions on each person's self-centred activities – the famous social contract.

The problem that the (fictitious) social contract solves is the (equally fictitious) problem of constraining the violence of all against all. Conversely, the problem that society solves for Hume is the problem of the natural poverty of sympathy:

> the problem of society is not a problem of limitation, but rather a problem of integration. To integrate sympathies is to make sympathy transcend its contradiction and natural partiality. Such an integration implies a positive moral world, and is bought about by the positive invention of such a world. (ES 26/39–40)

We are now in a position to see one reason why Deleuze spends so little time on Hume's definition of the passions and their various characteristics. The essence of morality will not be discovered by examining the advent of the passions, nor in the fact that moral judgements arise on their basis. It is as pointless to search for the ultimate grounds of morality as it is the origins of sensation. The problem of morality concerns the way in which our natural affective and moral particularities can be integrated into a social whole with everyone else's.

INSTINCTS AND INSTITUTIONS

What is the nature of this solution? There is only one possible answer: the invention of a set of artificial means that take up where nature leaves off. Taken together, the solution is nothing other than *society as such*, conceived as a moral world, a whole that integrates the particularities of our passions and engenders an extension of natural sympathy. The problem is a moral one, but the solution can only be a social and political one. But it would be equally true to say that morality – being based in sympathy – is from the start a social function, and that what is required is the integration of these various socialities. A society is only moral to the degree that it integrates the plural loci of sympathy around which the affective lives of families (in an extended sense of the world) turn.

This problematic is treated by Deleuze in a more straightforward, if compressed, fashion in a little text published the same year as *Empiricism and Subjectivity*, unsurprisingly entitled 'Instincts and Institutions'.[5] This text constitutes the introduction to an edited collection of the same name, in which Deleuze presents a range of extracts by other thinkers that engage with the opposition. As is often the case elsewhere in Deleuze's *oeuvre*, this shorter text helps us to understand the underlying motivations and problems that animate the larger work.

In 'Instincts and Institutions', Deleuze presents the Humean problematic we have been discussing on different, perhaps more general terrain.[6] The two titular concepts 'designate procedures of satisfaction'.[7] Both begin with the supposition of needs, drives, or what Deleuze here most often calls tendencies [*tendances*], but mark out two very different – apparently mutually exclusive – processes of their satisfaction.

The category of instinct describes a natural and unmediated passage from a need to its satisfaction, and in this sense is entirely utilitarian (though Deleuze will, somewhat strangely, assert that 'With instinct, nothing goes beyond utility, except beauty'[8]). The category of institution is instead necessarily artificial, and provides a mediated or indirect means for satisfaction. Any institution (marriage, the Church, etc.) is an 'organised system of means', nested inside more and more general institutions in turn (at least up to the level of the state, Deleuze suggests).

Now, whereas instinct is 'within' (in some, potentially problematic, sense)⁹ the individual, the institution is always prior to and presupposed by the individual and its search for satisfaction. The individual is always already within institutions. In the final analysis, then, the institution provides a *social* resolution of tendency.

On the level of a theory of society, though, the more specific opposition between the institution and the law appears. Whereas the former constitutes a positive, artificial construction, the law will 'place the positive outside the social (natural rights), and the social in the negative (contractual limitation)'.¹⁰ Laws are not here the correlate of instinct, though. Instinct, by virtue of the natural link it poses between need and satisfaction, requires neither institutions nor laws. Moreover, as in *Empiricism and Subjectivity*, Deleuze will argue that far from providing a means for the satisfaction of tendencies, the legal model can only be conceived as a constriction of these means. Hence the following interesting distinction, reminiscent of the approach espoused by the Marquis de Sade:

> tyranny is a regime in which there are many laws and few institutions; democracy is a regime in which there are many institutions, and few laws. Oppression becomes apparent when laws bear directly on people, and not on the prior institutions that protect them.¹¹

It is important to note that 'Instincts and Institutions' does not include an unambiguous endorsement of the latter concept by Deleuze. In particular, he notes that, by virtue of the indirect relationship between tendency and institution, we still need to account for how the two are actually brought together. Given, for example, the plurality of forms of marriage, why should any one of them come into play rather than any other in the search for sexual satisfaction? '[H]ow does the synthesis of tendencies and the object that satisfies them come about?'¹² There must be a third moment that can account for this:

The institution sends us back to a social activity that is constitutive of models of which we are not conscious, and which are not explained either by tendencies or utility, since human utility presupposes tendencies in the first place.[13]

The question thus becomes the following: 'What does the social mean with respect to tendencies?'[14]

GENERAL RULES

We will require a Humean version of the answer that Deleuze immediately gives to this question in this context: 'It means integrating circumstances into a system of anticipation, and internal factors into a system that regulates their appearance.'[15] We do not yet have the concepts at hand to provide much by way of detail here, though clearly it will involve the creation of an intermediary system of some kind, a point we will return to under the heading of 'determination'.

In 'Instincts and Institutions', Deleuze presents the two means of satisfaction as mutually exclusive. It is this that will lead him to the bizarre-seeming assertion that 'The Human is an animal decimating its species.'[16] He does not mean that we as a species are literally killing ourselves (which is nevertheless certainly true), but that as the process of institutionalisation progresses, we possess fewer and fewer instinctual means of satisfaction. The relationship of need and satisfaction has consequently become increasingly reversed: 'It is night because we sleep.'[17] Our species-being is the material consumed in the construction of society.

In *Empiricism and Subjectivity*, however, he argues that institutions are the instincts transformed by being amplified and extended. In keeping with the constructivist tenor of his reading of Hume, Deleuze emphasises the positivity of our relationship with what is natural; even there where nature requires the extension of culture, nature itself remains the fundamental element.[18] He makes this point, for instance, when he mentions the remarkable discussions of animal psychology that run through the *Treatise*: 'The distinction between nature and culture is precisely the distinction between simple and complex effects. Hume, throughout his work, shows a constant interest in the problems of animal psychology, perhaps because the animal is nature without culture' (ES 53/60).[19]

If we were to stay at the level of natural sympathy, human beings too would remain nothing more than animals. 'The affection of parents to their young proceeds from a peculiar instinct in animals, as well as in our species' (T 3.2.7.5), but what animals lack is any means to extend this affection beyond their local circumstances. We saw before that sympathy functions to produce a certain local generality (if this somewhat paradoxical phrase will be forgiven): certain neutral third-person points of view are produced, and thanks to them certain acts can be determined as good or evil due to the way in which the affects of pleasure and pain are made to circulate sympathetically.

But we have seen that this is not enough to constitute a general interest as such. We require something more than this locality, or rather, we require the same kind of effect but now writ large, a third-person point of view capable of being adopted by everyone. The means to establish this Hume calls *general rules*, and 'Hume's general rule is an institution' (ES 36/46).[20]

Consider the key case of property. Its value lies in the way that it makes the relationship between a person and their possessions a general feature of social life, and no longer an issue of any particular person or any particular object. Of this rule, Hume writes that:

when men, from their early education in society, have become sensible of the infinite advantages that result from it, and have besides acquired a new affection to company and conversation; and when they have observed, that the principal disturbance in society arises from those goods, which we call external, and from their looseness and easy transition from one person to another; they must seek for a remedy by putting these goods, as far as possible, on the same footing with the fixed and constant advantages of the mind and body. This can be done after no other manner, than by a convention entered into by all the members of the society to bestow stability on the possession of those external goods, and leave every one in the peaceable enjoyment of what he may acquire by his fortune and industry. By this means, every one knows what he may safely possess; and the passions are restrained in their partial and contradictory motions. (T 3.2.2.9)

So, the general rule that institutes private property is a social convention – that is, a socialised or institutionalised habit – that constitutes a neutral perspective from which the fact of possession now appears as an equally neutral social fact, rather than a matter of circumstance. And while, at least in this passage, Hume speaks of *constraining* the passions, for Deleuze it is rather a matter of *satisfying* them in a new way: 'In marriage, sexuality is satisfied; in property, greed' (ES 37/47).

To repeat, what is key here is the subsumption of the particular to the general in the rule. As Deleuze writes, before citing Hume, 'the general rule never indicates particular persons; it does not name owners. "Justice in her decisions, never regards the fitness or unfitness of objects to particular persons . . . the general rule [. . .] must extend to the whole society, and be inflexible either by spite or favour"' (ES 40/49, quoting T 3.2.3.3).

After introducing the figure of the general rule, Deleuze specifies that each rule possesses two poles. He identifies these as the rule's form and content, but we might equally designate them as its subjective and objective poles, anticipating the discussion yet to come on the nature of subjectivity. This first pole consists of conversation and convention. 'To be in a society', Deleuze writes, 'is first to substitute possible conversation for violence: the thought of each one represents in itself the thought of the others' (ES 29/41). His point is clear – without some minimal capacity to engage with others in common terms, there is no society. Every general rule must thus produce a certain intersubjective equanimity.

The same kind of stability must hold for the second, objective pole too, which Deleuze identifies with the rule of property and stable possession itself. We see the importance of the institution of property here, which is not merely one case of a general rule, but a kind of paradigm that can be extrapolated from. Without the set of conventions that maintain the past state of the social to some minimal degree, society is equally impossible. In the final analysis, equanimity in conversation is a conversation *about* property, about the stable order of objects, and the rule of property is 'the most necessary to the establishment of society' (T 3.2.2.12).

In a peculiar kind of presentiment of Hegel and Marx, for Hume our possessions are the mirrors in which our social relations are reflected back to us, and without them, intersubjectivity is ungrounded. Thus, in a remarkable phrase, Deleuze will assert: 'Hume thus finds property to be a phenomenon which is essentially political – in fact, the political phenomenon par excellence' (ES 30/42). He continues, writing that

> Property and conversation are joined at last, forming the two chapters of a social science. The general sense of the common interest must be *expressed* in order to be effective. Reason presents itself here as the conversation of proprietors. (ES 30/42)

A shared intersubjectivity and interobjectivity – such are the most general products of our social institutions, our general rules. On both sides, though, what is attained is a neutrality, a generality, a calm and neutral third-person point of view.

Let us note again a parallel with the principles of association, which also function in the first instance to extend what naturally belongs to experience. Association allows us to transcend the given (impressions of sensation and their concomitant ideas-images) in order that we can form beliefs; general rules allow us to transcend the given (natural sympathy) in order that we can form a stable and neutral perspective: 'The moral and social problem is how to go from real sympathies which exclude one another to a real whole which would include these sympathies. The problem is how to *extend* sympathy' (ES 28/40).

Deleuze will use Hume's term 'esteem' to name this neutral point of view, from which each person in a society appears as an equal to any other: already invoking the differential calculus in his first book, he writes that 'Esteem is the integral of sympathies; such is the foundation of justice' (ES 27/40). Justice is in turn only possible on the basis of the neutral point of view furnished by the ensemble of general rules. This explains Hume's frequent use of the phrase 'the rules of justice', and Deleuze's decision to include under the heading of 'justice' all general rules at this first level of operation.

CORRECTING THE PASSIONS: FROM GENERALITY TO THE GENERALISATION OF VIVACITY

If we follow the analogy with the mechanisms of belief further, we could expect to discover that this first application of general rules will be insufficient on its own to achieve the correction of natural sympathy – and this is exactly what Deleuze will argue, though the two corrections will bear an inverted sense.

In belief, a correction of the associative principles is required because these principles extend too far: we believe too many things. In morality, the problem is not that the general rules go too far, but they do too little. General rules produce a neutral, third-person perspective which founds the possibility of justice, by integrating the natural interests of each individual within the strictures of institutions. What is lost in this socialisation of subjects and objects is the vivacity of the passions that first infused the partial attachments of each person. I may now have an investment in all children living in good homes, but this investment is a pale facsimile of the love and joy I feel towards my own. More generally, 'sympathy, through general rules, has won the constancy, distance and uniformity of true moral judgment but has lost in vividness what it has gained in extension' (ES 40–1/50).

The function of general rules is the subsumption of the particular to the general, but society remains charged, nevertheless, by localised points of passional investment. As Deleuze notes, an interest in the well-being of another's children 'at least has the practical advantage, even when the heart is not in it, of being a general and immutable criterion, a third interest which does not depend on our interlocutors' (ES 29/41). But it remains the case that this interest must acquire 'from elsewhere the vividness that it lacks' (ES 29/41).

The means of correcting illegitimate beliefs was, let us recall, the fact that experience furnishes us with material that we can use to test the likelihood of our current beliefs; the mechanism of theoretical reason with respect to experience is thus *comparison*. In morality, no such mechanism exists, since the formation of a general rule already includes everybody and everything in principle (it is both a *rule* and *general*). The means to redress the affective neutrality of any given general rule will, and can only, be *other general rules*.

Let us consider again the case of property ownership. This institution provides a means to extend to everyone my sense that what I possess should remain my own. This is a rule that I will hold to be valid for all, but, as Deleuze says, my heart is not in it. The laptop that someone has left unattended at a table across from me at the library therefore tests my conviction: I could quite easily steal it and leave without anyone being the wiser. What is it that stops me from doing so?

The institution in question is what Hume calls *government*. Compared with the majority of people, who have only a rather loose commitment to the bond between strangers and their property, those who govern are deeply committed. As Hume writes,

There are the persons, whom we call civil magistrates, kings and their ministers, our governors and rulers, who being indifferent persons to the greatest part of the state, have no interest, or but a remote one, in any act of injustice; and being satisfied with their present condition, and with their part in society, have an immediate interest in every execution of justice, which is so necessary to the upholding of society. (T 3.2.7.7)

Not only is the government composed of people who like being in power and are attached to remaining there, the same people have no personal interest in stealing laptops in libraries, these interests being invested in the institution of government itself. These people are not, however, somehow a kingdom within a kingdom, somehow exempt from the fortunes of the passions. It is the very nature of the affective life of human being that makes them – *given the position they are in* – so effective in charging justice with the vivacity that it lacks on its own. Those who govern have an interest in keeping things the way that they are, and will thus look with a baleful eye on anyone upsetting the status quo.

How does this affect me as I consider the laptop out of the corner of my eye? While the rule of property gives me a general but affectively weak reason to not steal it, the rule of law embodied by the state is something with which I do have a direct affective relationship. Those in government, 'then, are not only induced to observe those rules in their own conduct, but also to constrain others to a like regularity, and inforce the dictates of equity through the whole society' (T 3.2.7.7). And when disputes arise – as they always will, given the patchwork composition of society with its irreducible centres of sympathetic investment – then given the fact that this third party exists whose own investments are in the maintenance of the rules of justice themselves, I can trust (to some degree) that they will be impartial.

By means of these two advantages, in the execution and decision of justice, men acquire a security against each others weakness and passion, as well as against their own, and under the shelter of their governors, begin to taste at ease the sweets of society and mutual assistance. (T 3.2.7.8)

It is worth repeating the fact that, like justice, government is a general rule, that is, an invented institution that allows for the transcendence of partiality. 'Justice and government have the same source; "they are contrived to remedy like inconveniences": the one simply invents extension, the other, vivacity' (ES 42/51, quoting T 3.2.8.3). At the same time, there remains a difference in kind here, akin to that found between nature and society. On this point, Deleuze is particularly clear, writing of the distinction between justice and government that

> We find here the principle of all serious political philosophy. True morality does not address itself to children in the family but rather to adults in the state. It does not involve the change of human nature but the invention of artificial and objective conditions in order for the bad aspects of this nature not to triumph. This invention, for Hume, as for the entire eighteenth century, will be political and only political. (ES 41/50)

THE POSSIBLE AND THE REAL: THE PLACE OF THE IMAGINATION IN MORALITY

But now, we need to note a fact that the two regimes of general rules do not allow us to explain: there is more than one form of government, and more than one way in which the stability of possession can be assured. Beyond the fact of this variety, there is also the fact of the imagination: I can always formulate hypothetical institutions that would differ from those that exist, and I can always raise problems that existing institutions cannot themselves resolve.

For instance, Deleuze likes to invoke a question Hume poses in a footnote to a discussion of possession through occupation:

> Two Grecian colonies, leaving their native country, in search of new feats, were informed that a city near them was deserted by its inhabitants. To know the truth of this report, they dispatched at once two messengers, one from each colony; who finding on their approach, that their information was true, begun a race together

with an intention to take possession of the city, each of them for his countrymen. One of these messengers, finding that he was not an equal match for the other, launched his spear at the gates of the city, and was so fortunate as to fix it there before the arrival of his companion. This produced a dispute betwixt the two colonies, which of them was the proprietor of the empty city and this dispute still subsists among philosophers. (T 3.2.3.4n15)

The problem this passage raises for Hume is whether or not lodging a spear in the gate of the city is itself sufficient to claim possession of the city. On one level – that of association – there is literally no way to justify an answer either way. Hume continues by confessing that 'For my part I find the dispute impossible to be decided, and that because the whole question hangs upon the fancy, which in this case is not possessed of any precise or determinate standard, upon which it can give sentence' (T 3.2.3.4n15). He then adds a series of related questions: what if the two colonies had only sent regular citizens rather than messengers? Would that be enough to establish ownership? And why the gates rather than one of the walls? And anyway, why wouldn't merely touching the gates be enough? Why should the spear be the determining factor? Similar questions arise today around the planting of flags and public assertion of possession – concerning the Arctic Circle, for example, or portions of the ocean, but also the lunar surface. Moral life always unfolds in immediate proximity to a host of 'bizarre questions which seem somehow familiar to us: Just how far can we possess the seas? Why in a system of justice is the soil more important than the surface? But then why is the paint more important than the canvas?'[21]

In fact, this indeterminacy is more apparent than real, or, to be more precise, it is only one facet of a situation that invites a positive and constructive response. In what way? We should not expect that the first general rule that institutes stable possession is in effect in some indeterminate form. There is no generic 'property ownership' that is not already embodied in more specific general rules: occupancy, for example, or immediate possession ('finders keepers'). That is, the stability of possession – like every institution – only exists in various determinate forms.

So, in truth, there is not one general rule pertaining to stable possession but always a multiplicity: 'the general rule, that possession must be stable, is not applied by particular judgments, but by other general rules' (T 3.2.3.3). The real question we find here is therefore not the negative one: 'how can I decide without any criteria what constitutes possession?' It is instead this: 'what is the source of this variety in institutional models?'

The answer is the imagination itself, which is nothing other than the locus for the production of images under the effects of the principles of association. Unconstrained, I can imagine a whole sequence of property regimes as fantastic and diverse as the fictions detailed in Calvino's *Invisible Cities*. Thus Deleuze writes:

> The imagination is revealed as a veritable production of extremely diverse *models*: when drives are reflected in an imagination submitted to the principles of association, institutions are determined by the figures traced by the drives according to the circumstances. This does not mean that the imagination is in its essence active but only that it *rings out*, and *resonates*. The institution is the figure. (ES 39/48–9)

This is a key passage in Deleuze's explication, albeit a compressed one. Leaving aside the question of circumstance, which we will deal with in the chapter on subjectivity, what does it tell us?

We know that the imagination is not an active faculty that we could identify with human agency itself. At the most basic level, it is nothing other than a disorganised collection of images (ideas) that it uniquely and solely produces. What transforms this into a system are the principles of association, which give rise to a network of complex ideas or beliefs. Now, we also know that these beliefs can never constitute knowledge in the strong sense of the word. At best they can be judged to be highly probable. In other words, what peoples the imagination are possible images of the world, or, better, *images of possible worlds*.

We have seen that the passions are nothing other than impressions of reflection. To recall Hume's definition, an 'idea of pleasure or pain, when it returns upon the soul, produces the new impressions of desire and aversion, hope and fear, which may properly be called impressions of reflexion, because derived from it' (T 1.1.2.1). When we first presented this point, it was as though the reflective medium of the imagination was a clear and neutral surface, a particularly tranquil lake or particularly pristine mirror. In truth, though, it is always already subject to the processes of association, so the reflections of the primary impressions of pleasure and pain are necessarily refracted in accordance with the existing structure of the mind. The images of possible worlds that populate the imagination thus necessarily give structure to the impressions of reflection at the moment of their formation.

But here the more important fact is that the converse also holds: 'We associate our ideas because we have passions' (ES 58/63). The ideas on which association works are not neutral, but charged with the affects of pleasure and pain that arise from the passions. However bucolic the examples of billiards and backgammon may be, they can mislead us into thinking of the production of beliefs as entirely untroubled, upper-middle class. The truth is that there is no association in the mind that is not motivated in a basic sense by the passions and the affects they give rise to.

This remarkable account that draws together everything we have already seen about belief and morality leads to a concise conclusion: institutions are figures for the resolution of needs whose architect is habitual association. What ensures their real construction, though, is not association, but the fact of affect and the experience of sympathy. For this reason, we can talk about a schematism proper to morality but produced in the imagination. The possible rules that could satisfy the drives – that is, induce positive affect in my engagement in the world – are images of possible institutions, *imaginary institutions*. The real institutions that come to be are first born in the troubled waking dreams of the subject.

It is important to recall that this sequential way of presenting the matter is merely heuristic, and that everything takes place together in the mind: the production of institutional models is oriented and motivated by the affective context that the subject finds itself in, but even more basically the extension of sympathy and the association of ideas are intertwined processes. Association gives to morality stable connections with which to work, while morality provides the mind with the motivation to produce associations.

Everything we have just seen about stable possession also holds for the other case we have examined, *government*. Not only are there a variety of forms of government, there are also and more importantly for Hume a variety of means for our loyalty to the government to be established. We could invoke a stable rule of succession, for instance, or transparent elections, or the rule of a country across many centuries by the same family. All of these are means by which the government can become that stable entity to which we can become loyal. Like the variety of means for stable possession, these are engendered in the imagination under the guidance of the principles of association, under the impetus of the passions, and brought into reality in the context of social life.

Finally, Deleuze will write that 'the true moralist is the legislator' (ES 29/41). Legislation here is the act that carries us from image to institution, and, despite the novelty of the passional association we have just seen, it is legislation that is the true invention, and 'the true inventors are not technologists but rather the legislators. They are not Asclepius or Bacchus but rather Romulus and Theseus' (ES 29/41).

The problem that Deleuze takes these determinations to resolve is nothing other than the problem that 'Instincts and Institutions' poses without resolving. What kind of activity, 'constitutive of models of which we are not conscious, and which are not explained either by tendencies or utility'[22] might we invoke? How can the gap be closed between the general rule and the particular people it presents itself to as a means of resolution? The answer, we now see, is the fabulating imagination itself.

HUME'S POLITICAL ECONOMY

The discussion of the extensive and corrective uses of general rules, and the imaginative-determinative function of association are brought together – and themselves extended – by Deleuze in his short but remarkable discussion of Hume's political economy which closes the second chapter of *Empiricism and Subjectivity*. In fact, the chapter closes with the table shown in Table 1 (ES 46/54).[23]

Table 1 Summary of Hume's general rules

A. Justice	B. Government	C. Commerce
1. Content of the general rule: the stability of possession	1. Support of the general rule: loyalty to the government	1. Complement to the general rule: the prosperity of commerce
2. Determination of the general rule by general rules: immediate possession, occupation, etc.	2. Determination of the support: long-term possession, accession, etc.	2. Determination of the complement: monetary circulation, capital, etc.
3. Correction of the preceding determination by general rules: promises, transfer	3. Correction: resistance	3. Correction: taxes, the public service, etc.

So far, we have only considered the first four cells. We have just seen that the general rule that institutes the stability of possession comes into being not in brute form but as a variety of particular general rules. This, again, is why Deleuze speaks of property as the *content* of the general rule. We have also seen that all primary general rules extend our sympathetic engagement with the world, but at the cost of weakening their vivacity. For this reason, secondary general rules are required to reinvigorate the first rank, and in the case of stable possession, this is found in the institution of government, and in our immediate investment in not falling afoul of the people who form the government, whose own immediate investment is in the longevity of the government itself.

As Deleuze's table indicates, though, this is only part of the story. Two further corrections will be required. Let us start with the first row, which suggests the need for a complement to the general rule of property in addition to its support in government. What is at issue here?

> Up to now, a first series of rules has given to interest an extension and a generality that interest did not have on its own: through this, possession has turned into property, and stability of possession has been achieved. A second series of rules has given the general rule the presence and vivacity that it did not have by itself. But the obstacles which society had to conquer are not only the instability of goods and the abstract character of the general interest. Society is also faced with a scarcity of goods. And stability, far from surmounting this obstacle, aggravates it further since it provides possession with conditions favourable to the formation of large properties. (ES 43/51)

The institution of government is the object of an affective investment (loyalty), but this way of organising social investment tends by itself to consolidate property in a very unequal way – the more durable the rule of possession is, the less property will circulate in society as a whole. This in turn tends to destabilise the politically organised regime of justice. In the most immediate sense, then, the problem lies with the chance distribution of objects. As Hume drily puts it, 'persons and possessions must often be very ill adjusted' (T 3.2.4.1). Some countries possess enormous natural resources, and others none at all, and the only alternative to the warfare that would destroy societies over this differential scarcity is a stable means of distribution.

The primary example both Hume and Deleuze use is the ownership of land. As Hume notes in his classic essay 'Of Interest',

> When a people have emerged ever so little from a savage state, and their numbers have encreased beyond the original multitude, there must immediately arise an inequality of property; and while some possess large tracts of land, others are confined within narrow limits, and some are entirely without any landed property.[24]

The institutions of property ownership which compose the rules of justice thus require a supplement of a kind quite different to what is provided by government. Instead of providing vivacity, it will have to introduce a certain dynamism into the bond that justice instantiates and government reinforces.

To illustrate this point, Deleuze chooses the example of interest, but the case of the merchant is perhaps clearer and certainly more straightforward. The problem that exists is the unequal distribution of possessions. The figure of the merchant, and more broadly what we could call the institution of merchandry, is a means to break down this static inequality. Hume calls the merchant 'one of the most useful races of men, who serve as agents between those parts of the state, that are wholly unacquainted, and are ignorant of each other's necessities',[25] before describing the following scenario:

> In this province, grass rises in abundance: The inhabitants abound in cheese, and butter, and cattle; but want bread and corn, which, in a neighbouring province, are in too great abundance for the use of the inhabitants. One man discovers this. He brings corn from the one province and returns with cattle; and supplying the wants of both, he is, so far, a common benefactor. As the people encrease in numbers and industry, the difficulty of their intercourse encreases: The business of the agency

or merchandize becomes more intricate; and divides, subdivides, compounds, and mixes to a greater variety. In all these transactions, it is necessary, and reasonable, that a considerable part of the commodities and labour should belong to the merchant, to whom, in a great measure, they are owing.[26]

Not only does the case of merchandry illustrate very clearly the role that such an institution of commerce plays in modulating the rule of stable possession to avoid the problems that it gives rise to, it also includes a great example of what Deleuze means by the determination of the general rule. We do not find a generic merchant, but always particular exemplars, and these themselves proliferate in the face of proliferating interests. Like justice and government themselves, commerce is not comprised of a single general rule, but a multitude of different forms, engendered by the refraction of the passions in the imagination. There is no one rule which invests us in the success of commerce, but many. So, commerce too is the object of a determination, the *determination of the complement*. These rules give to us the means to satisfy our particular interests in the general context of social life.[27]

Before we turn to the last row of the table, a further point about complementarity. Note that commerce is for Hume a corrective not to government but to justice. There even appears to be a tension between the aims of government and those of commerce. Where government more tightly yokes property and owner together, commerce provides a regulated means for breaking this bond. There is even one sense, as Hume indicates in 'Of Interest', in which commerce is independent of and primary in relation to government. The passage cited above continues by noting that

Those who possess more land than they can labour, employ those who possess none, and agree to receive a determinate part of the product. Thus the *landed* interest is immediately established; nor is there any settled government, however rude, in which affairs are not on this footing.[28]

The intricacy and breadth of this account is surely impressive, but there remains one further corrective deployment of general rules that must be noted, composing the bottom row of Deleuze's little table. Deleuze will call this third moment the *correction of the determination*. Again, as with the first two moments, we must keep in mind that we are not dealing with a discrete sequence of steps: 'We must therefore in the case of the general rule distinguish three dimensions which are nonetheless simultaneous: its *establishment*, its *determination*, and its *correction*' (ES 40/50).

What precisely requires correction here? The problem is not one of extension without vivacity, or of an institutionalisation of a certain instability. We know that the relationship between the general rule and its determination concerns a proliferation of institutional models thanks to the mediation of the fabulating imagination. Notice though that the institutions that are produced on the basis of this fabulation, despite being specific determinations of the general rule, continue to manifest a particular kind of generality. They are formulated not in response to real people's needs, but on the basis of imagined possible states of the world. So the question is this: 'how can the lack of adequation between real persons and possible situations be *corrected*?' (ES 40/49). True, the advent of the merchandry creates new ways to satisfy particular needs or interests, but this does not mean that the merchant will be equipped to deal with every interest. The dairy farmer, the publisher and the jeweller all need to sell their wares, but a book fair is neither a delicatessen nor a jewellery store.

The solution, unsurprisingly, is the invention of more general rules. In the first column, we encounter rules that correct the determinate instances of stable possession. The problem they address is that the concrete institutions in question provide us with quite broad rules that constitute possession, and by themselves they are not directly applicable to any particular case. It is not possible, Hume notes, to 'transfer the property of ten bushels of corn, or five hogsheads of wine, by the mere expression and consent; because these are only general terms and have no direct relation to any particular heap of corn, or barrels of wine' (T 3.2.5.8). How exactly can the ownership of a beloved first edition of Freud's *Interpretation of Dreams* be transferred to a friend? 'A man, dangerously wounded, who promises a competent sum to a surgeon to cure him, would certainly be bound to performance; though the case be not so much different from that of one, who promises a sum to a robber' (T 3.2.5.16) – but what constitutes the real difference between the two cases? The matter only gets more complicated when the property at issue is not a physical thing, but, for instance, a favour (T 3.2.5.9).

How to leap this gap? We need new rules that will allow for an intertwining of the somewhat generic determinations and particular cases with respect to the modification of the subject–object, owner–property pair. Deleuze emphasises two of these new corrective rules: *promising* and what he just calls 'transfers' but which Hume will mostly describe as *transference of property by consent*. Both are rules that institute an obligation of a certain kind, one that we are invested in through the mechanism of property ownership itself and its invigorated state form. Moreover, in both cases, the rule in question is immediately applicable to the case at hand: when I promise, I do not do so as a generic subject, but as myself – something that is made obvious by the fact that if I break the promise, I am the immediate recipient of the disgrace effected by such an act.[29]

The two cases are distinguished on the basis of presence and absence: a promise allows for the transfer of something absent to someone else who is present, while transfer by consent allows me to give something that is currently in my possession to someone who is absent, often by using an artifice appropriate to the transfer: 'Thus the giving the keys of a granary is understood to be the delivery of the corn contained in it' (T 3.2.4.2).

Now, the case of government is particularly revealing here. We have seen that the state is required in order to infuse the rule of property with a degree of vivacity sufficient to make strangers care about my property rights as much as their own. Equally, the state, by virtue of its neutrality, appears as the rightful arbiter of disputes between individuals and their particular interests.

Now, facile and ahistorical invocations of neutral, anodyne political rule should always give us pause; the truth is anything but easy. The history of government is not the history of stability, even-handedness and trust, but of power, coercion and violence, implied and all too real. Hume too was aware of this fact, and for this reason his account of government does not stop at invoking its benefits. There is a very real gap between the various general rules that make us loyal to the government, and real people who engage them. This gap is redressed, according to Hume, not by the government engendering even more ways to endorse or believe in it. The proliferations of determinative forms cannot overcome this gap, because every form of loyalty to the government is instituted at some distance from particular people.

What is required are general rules that will allow people in their particularity to resist the government when its rule becomes unjust. If 'nothing is more essential to public interest, than the preservation of public liberty' (T 3.2.10.17), should a government begin to act in a way that undoes this public interest, it becomes the object of a legitimate practical and critical redress. As Deleuze puts it,

> If rulers [. . .], instead of acquiring an immediate interest in the administration of justice, were to subject the administration of falsified justice to their own immediate passions, then and only then would resistance be legitimate, in the name of a general rule. (ES 42–3/51)

Deleuze emphasises the very specific circumstances in which active resistance would be justified for Hume. For the latter, the most important thing to realise about this gap between government and individual is that the right of resistance is never absent: 'It is certain, therefore, that in all our notions of morals we never entertain such an absurdity as that of passive obedience, but make allowances for resistance in the more flagrant instances of tyranny and oppression' (T 3.2.9.4).

The final cell of the table to discuss concerns the correction of the rule of commerce, and, as both of the examples Deleuze lists indicate (state service and taxation), this correction involves the precise way in which government takes part in the institutions of commerce for Hume. As with property and government, the corrective rule here deals with the incommensurability between determinate institutions and real individuals.

The problem precipitated by the institution(s) of commerce is, unsurprisingly, new forms of inequality, now deriving from the unequal distribution of money rather than possessions. It is certainly the case, Deleuze insists, that government 'finds in commerce the possible affirmation of its power and the real condition of its subjects' prosperity' (ES 45/53), but without correction, these institutions can easily function to undermine this prosperity instead. This correction is supplied by bending the institutions of commerce more closely to the institutions of the government. Deleuze gives us two examples: taxation and the public service. In the first case, a portion of profit made through commerce is returned to the government to facilitate its goal of reinforcing the public interest; the second concerns commercial activities performed in the name of the state itself.

In sum, then, not only are all general rules subject to a redoubling that provides them with the vivacity that they sacrifice for their generality, they are also *determined* according to the models provided by the understanding, and this determination is *corrected* from the point of view of concrete cases. *Invention always calls for imaginative construction and the counterbalance of a corrective casuistry.*

This table has the appearance of constituting a full account of all general rules, but this is far from the case. Consider the corrective rule of consensual transfer. Like the rule of stable possession that it corrects, there are various models we could imagine and institute – different legal avenues, various qualifications of consent, and so on. Another obvious example is the corrective rule of taxation. While its purpose is to ameliorate the tendency of commerce to entrench inequality, it can equally have the opposite effect. There is not one institution of taxation but a great many, and each of these determinations in turn would require correction by others in order to avoid the deleterious effects of regressive taxation.[30] With respect to a third example, promises, Hume himself points to the subsequent determinations that can arise: 'As the obligation of promises is an invention for the interest of society, it is warped into as many different forms as that interest requires, and even runs into contradictions rather than lose sight of its object' (T 3.2.5.15).

So the truth of the matter is much rather that, beginning with the cornerstone of stable possession, the history of societies unfolds according to an ongoing, ramified process of invention, where each new institution calls for more invention yet again – an efflorescence of novel means and their modifications.

THE PRIMACY OF PRACTICAL REASON

The whole complex of artificial means that institutes the social order as a regime of general interests and their satisfaction is the object of a practical reason. In social life as in the life of the individual, theoretical reason is subordinated to the passions and their amplification and resolution – that is, to practical reason.

Following Hume, and here we return to the theme with which this chapter began, Deleuze will present the primacy of practical reason from both a negative and a positive point of view.

The negative point of view concerns the powerlessness of theoretical reason. On the one hand, the associations of ideas constitute a set of tendencies in the mind that make beliefs possible, but this is all. They have absolutely no capacity to bring about any course of action. In particular, a cause and effect relationship tells us nothing about means and ends. We have already observed that this association runs in both directions, valorising neither pole, while the relationship between ends and means is unidirectional, and laden with (affective, passional) significance. Deleuze is particularly clear on this point:

> for a cause to be considered as a means, the effect which it brings about must interest us, that is, the idea of the effect must first of all be posited as an end for our action. The means exceeds the cause: the effect must be thought of as a good, the subject who projects it must have a tendency to achieve it. The relation of means to end is not merely causal; it is rather a kind of utility. The useful is defined by its appropriation or by its disposition 'to promote a good.' A cause is a means only for a subject that tends to achieve the effect of this cause. (ES 141/125)

On the other hand, reason itself is no less effective. We know that reason is a habituated comparative mechanism, able to qualify beliefs as probable or improbable. So reason itself is not a principle of human nature or association, but neither is it itself a belief constituted by association. What then is it? There is only one answer left: an impression of reflection, that is, a *passion*.

Hume deploys a first sceptical line of argument about reason in order to foreclose any possibility that it is as rational, calculating agents that we act:

> The chief spring or actuating principle of the human mind is pleasure or pain; and when these sensations are removed, both from our thought and feeling, we are, in a great measure, incapable of passion or action, of desire or volition. (T 3.3.1.2)

However, his second line of argument that locates reason as a habit constituted through reflection is not sceptical, and its goal is to give back to reason what was illegitimately occluded in classical rationalism. This is what will lead Deleuze to say that

> Reason is a kind of feeling. Consequently, just as the method of philosophy goes from the absence of an idea to the presence of

an impression, similarly the theory of reason moves also from a kind of skepticism to a kind of positivism. It moves from a skepticism of reason to a positivism of feeling, in which case the latter includes reason as a reflection of feeling in the qualified mind. (ES 14/30)

The fact that reason is the result of reflection in the mind will be an important ingredient of Deleuze's account of subjectivity in Hume. But beyond this point itself lies an even more important positive claim. If practical reason is and must be primary for Hume, this is because it provides the only possible protection against the plague of fantasies that attend belief and reason on their own terms. Here, we can repurpose a diagram that Deleuze uses more than thirty years later in his last sole-authored work, *The Fold: Leibniz and the Baroque* (Figure 1).[31]

On their own terms, and despite the corrective of reason, beliefs remain ungrounded and ultimately unjustifiable. Because there is no fixed ground of experience, no split pin that could hold its repetitions together, we have no way of knowing if we

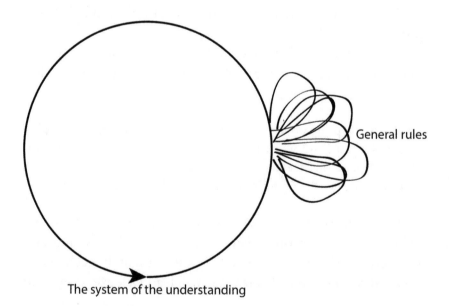

The system of the understanding

Figure 1 Practical reason as bond

are spiralling in the void or not. Worse, the imagination can always fabulate fictitious repetitions to support the most insane hypotheses.

But beliefs are never isolated, never on their own terms. The moral world is always the context in which they are formulated and played out, or, better, this world provides beliefs with an *artificial ground*, providing them something they could never attain on their own. In place of the empty forms of the Cartesian *cogito* and the Kantian transcendental unity of apperception, the mirroring Leibnizian monad and Spinoza's determinate degree of God's essence, is the shifting multiplicity of general rules, which is to say, society itself. 'Reason can always be brought to bear, but it is brought to bear on a pre-existing world and presupposes an antecedent ethics and an order of ends' (ES 18/33).

For Deleuze, it is only in abstract terms that we could ever oppose the individual and the social in Hume. There is rather a continuum, one that runs from my particular and limited sphere of sympathetic relations and the network of complex ideas I possess due to the principles of association, to the ongoing movement of integration with an eye to a whole – that is, to the social institutions as the horizon for human being. Given the apparent solipsism that the Humean picture of belief presents us with, this is all the more remarkable. For while we might need to insist with Hume the philosophical psychologist on the absolute inaccessibility of the in-itself in the sphere of knowledge, 'Hume is a moralist and a sociologist before being a psychologist' (ES 1/21). More to the point:

> We should not, in fact, forget that two points of view coexist in Hume: the passions and the understanding present themselves [. . .] as two distinct parts. By itself, though, *the understanding is only the process of the passions on their way to socialization.* Sometimes we see that the understanding and the passions constitute two separate problems, but at other times, we see that the understanding is subordinated to the passions. (ES 2/22)

73

RECAPITULATION

The trajectory that leads us from pleasure and pain to the primacy of practical reason is, as we have seen, a fairly complicated one. It will therefore be worth recapitulating its major moments:

1. We possess passions, which are impressions of reflection, ultimately grounded in original impressions of pain and pleasure. These passions – primarily, love and hatred, pride and shame – constitute moral judgements, which 'prompt us to praise or blame' (ES 23/37).

2. We are naturally sympathetic to others near to us and like us: the family, not the individual, comes first. Sympathy names our attachment to these others through an affective mirroring, which gives rise in us to the emotions we experience in them.

3. Sympathy is limited in scope, but is extended through general rules. These are social institutions like marriage, or property ownership, which allow us to integrate our particular interests into a general interest. These institutions are artificial, that is, *inventions*. 'Moral conscience is', therefore, 'a determination of psychological consciousness; it is psychological consciousness apprehended exclusively under the aspect of its inventive power' (ES 28–9/41).[32]

4. General rules, conceived in this way, are affectively limited. Their lack of vivacity is corrected for through the invention of further general rules that intertwine the general interest and our particular affective investments. The theoretical limits of the basic conception of general rules is overcome by seeing that every such general rule (like property ownership) is always multiple in fact, and that other general rules come to bridge the gap between their generality and the specific cases that they come to bear on.

Finally, it is worth recalling and finessing the equation of the social, the political, and the moral I presented earlier. Rather than simply identifying the three, it would be better to say that morality is a factor present in nature, society and politics, each time in a slightly different role. The moral world, finally, can be found at each of these three moments. In nature, morality consists in sympathy in its limited deployment and in the oligarchy of the passions. In society, natural moral sentiment appears as the kernels around which institutions are formed, and the material from which these institutions are constructed. With the deployment of the imagination and the corrective general rules, morality appears in a third guise, as a reflexive and critical insistence on the singular and the exception. This is the third act in the tale of morality. There, we no longer appear as children, blind and passionate, yet to be inducted into the warp and weft of social reality, but as adults who possess the inventive character of human being fully and by right. So, in another sense, the moral world is an *achievement*, and the nature–society–politics sequence only names the stages that must be passed through in order to obtain it.

NOTES

1. Any sense that the issue is merely terminological is immediately banished when one reads, on the back cover of the English translation, that '*Empiricism and Subjectivity* took a significant step toward the idea of ethics without morality.'
2. Hume also seems – very quickly and in passing (T 2.3.9.8) – to introduce a third category of passions, which are immediately produced in the mind without any need for the initial impression of pleasure or pain. As Deleuze has it, 'there are passions born of their principles, without these principles causing them to go through preliminary pleasures and pains' (ES 116). Here, Norman Kemp Smith's account, according to which these constitute a class of 'primary' passions ('sheerly instinctive [. . .] arising from a natural impulse or instinct'), remains a convincing one on its own terms (Norman Kemp Smith, *The Philosophy*

of David Hume (Basingstoke: Palgrave, [1941] 2005), 168). But because Deleuze does not draw any broader consequence from the direct/indirect distinction – while noting the novelty of Hume's approach, which does not try to derive one from the other (ES 118) – we can leave this aside here.

3. David Fate Norton, 'The Foundations of Morality in Hume's *Treatise*', in *The Cambridge Companion to Hume*, ed. David Fate Norton (Cambridge: Cambridge University Press, 1993), 165.

4. See also T 3.2.1.18: 'A man naturally loves his children better than his nephews, his nephews better than his cousins, his cousins better than strangers, where every thing else is equal.'

5. Gilles Deleuze, 'Instincts and Institutions', in *Desert Islands and Other Texts*, ed. David Lapoujade, trans. Michael Taormina (New York: Semiotext(e), 2004), 19–21.

6. I agree with Joe Hughes that the framing of the question here moves us much closer to Bergson than to Hume, and that the collection of texts itself, which includes very little material from the latter, presents the solution (integration through institutions) in an essentially Bergsonian fashion. See Joe Hughes, *Philosophy After Deleuze* (London: Bloomsbury, 2012), 124–5. That said, we must also recognise Bergson's presence in *Empiricism and Subjectivity* itself at key moments. One of these concerns the status of time (ES 100/92–3), which we will return to below; another concerns precisely the problem of the fit between need (or drive) and the institution (ES 39/48).

7. Deleuze, 'Instincts and Institutions', 19.

8. Deleuze, 'Instincts and Institutions', 20.

9. Deleuze's somewhat muted critique of the concept of instinct here turns around the fact that, when we examine it carefully, it seems to turn into a form of species intelligence, but one that consequently 'implies a period of time too long for the individual to live, and experiments which it would not survive' (Deleuze, 'Instincts and Institutions', 21).

10. Deleuze, 'Instincts and Institutions', 19.

11. Deleuze, 'Instincts and Institutions', 20.

12. Deleuze, 'Instincts and Institutions', 21.

13. Deleuze, 'Instincts and Institutions', 20.

14. Deleuze, 'Instincts and Institutions', 21.

15. Deleuze, 'Instincts and Institutions', 21.
16. Deleuze, 'Instincts and Institutions', 21.
17. Deleuze, 'Instincts and Institutions', 21.
18. This theme, found throughout *Empiricism and Subjectivity*, appears to be contradicted at one point by Deleuze himself, when he writes that 'Because human beings do not have instincts, because instincts do not enslave them to the actuality of a pure present, they have liberated the formative power of their imagination, and they have placed their drives in an immediate and direct relation to it' (ES 39/49). This remark is found in a passage that at moments duplicates the letter of 'Instincts and Institutions', and it is therefore possible that Deleuze here weaves a part of that text into his argument. The fact remains, though, that there is a natural and unmediated satisfaction of the drives in sympathy according to Hume. That is to say that there is indeed something akin to instinct, something that can even be assimilated to the principles of human nature as such if we extend our discussion onto epistemological terrain as well. We will not aim to resolve this tension here, but instead proceed on the basis of Deleuze's much more common invocation of the social as the extension and correction of the natural.
19. In addition to a great many remarks in passing, Hume devotes three separate sections of the *Treatise* to animal psychology, one in each book and on topics exemplary of those books: 'Of the Reason of Animals' (T 1.3.16), 'Of the Pride and Humility of Animals' (T 2.1.7) and 'Of the Love and Hatred of Animals' (T 3.2.7).
20. Hume uses this phrase throughout the whole of the *Treatise*, and while its overall meaning – as, essentially, any extensive use of reflection – is the same throughout, the term is less than apposite in some cases. I agree with Thomas Hearn when he writes that, with respect to epistemological questions where what is involved is 'a generalizing propensity of the imagination which extends the scope of judgments or opinions under certain conditions', the term is 'hardly the best way to designate the notion that Hume is employing here' (Thomas K. Hearn, '"General Rules" in Hume's *Treatise*', *Journal of the History of Philosophy*, 8:4 (1970), 408). While Deleuze occasionally notes the broader sense of the phrase

'general rule' (e.g. ES 7/25), and sometimes explicitly speaks of the habits produced by the principles of association in these terms (e.g. ES 144/127), he for the most part reserves it for the discussion of morality in Hume, where both parts of the phrase are clearly *à propos*.

21. Gilles Deleuze, 'Hume', in *Desert Islands and Other Texts*, ed. David Lapoujade, trans. Michael Taormina (New York: Semiotext(e), 2004), 162.

22. Deleuze, 'Instincts and Institutions', 20.

23. The English translation of this table is partial and somewhat misleading. In particular, the choice of 'specification' (a word that Hume never to my knowledge uses) for *détermination* is problematic, erasing as it does Deleuze's earlier discussion of the determination of general rules. For example, he writes that 'We must therefore in the case of the general rule distinguish three dimensions which are nonetheless simultaneous: its *establishment*, its *determination*, and its *correction*' (ES 40/48). The matter is not helped, unfortunately, by the fact that throughout the body of the text, the word *détermination* is translated in both ways. The table is also missing the header row in the English version, which makes it harder to grasp it as a summary of the preceding chapter.

24. Hume, 'Of Interest', in *Essays: Moral, Political and Literary* (New York: Cosimo, 2006), 2.4.7; 305.

25. Hume, 'Of Interest', 2.4.10; 308.

26. Hume, 'Of Interest', 2.4.10; 308.

27. Deleuze considers an analogous correction in relation to the institution of marriage (ES 51/58–9). Marriage functions as a means to satisfy sexual desire. Like all institutions, though, there is not one form of marriage, but 'thousands' (ES 37/47) produced through the creative and reflective apparatus of the imagination. However, a gap remains between even the most particular form of marriage and real individuals. More precisely, 'a wife cannot give to the one who loves her perfect certainty and security: anatomy precludes it. The husband can never be sure that the children are his own' (ES 51/58). To bridge this gap, another corrective institution must be engendered: 'Reflected in the imagination, this uncertainty becomes sublimated, takes on a social and

cultural content, and appears as the requirement for specifically feminine virtues: a woman, to the extent that she is the object of a possible passion, must always remain chaste, modest and decent' (ES 51/58).

28. Hume, 'Of Interest', 2.4.7; 305.

29. Hume comes very close, in his discussion of promising, to formulating a nascent version of speech act theory, when he notes that 'since every new promise imposes a new obligation of morality on the person who promises, and since this new obligation arises from his will; it is one of the most mysterious and incomprehensible operations that can possibly be imagined, and may even be compared to TRANSUBSTANTIATION, or HOLY ORDERS [I mean so far, as holy orders are suppos'd to produce the indelible character. In other respects they are only a legal qualification.], where a certain form of words, along with a certain intention, changes entirely the nature of an external object, and even of a human nature. But though these mysteries be so far alike, it is very remarkable, that they differ widely in other particulars, and that this difference may be regarded as a strong proof of the difference of their origins' (T 3.2.5.15).

30. Hume's observations on this matter are found in 'Of Taxes', in *Essays: Moral, Political and Literary* (New York: Cosimo, 2006), 2.3; 349–54.

31. Adapted from Gilles Deleuze, *The Fold: Leibniz and the Baroque*, trans. Tom Conley (London: Athlone, 1993), p. 26.

32. The original here reads *'la conscience morale est une détermination de la conscience psychologique'*. Boundas translates both uses of the French *conscience* as 'conscience', but in doing so obscures the fact that psychological consciousness is not inventive, and has no moral orientation of its own. In other words, for Hume there is nothing that answers to the name of 'psychological conscience'.

4

The Madness of Thought and the Delirium of Practical Reason

The long discussion of morality, society and political economy in the previous chapter led us to remark the primacy of practical reason, and the concomitant practical neutrality of theoretical reason. It might seem strange then to return to imagination and the understanding in the wake of this. If we must do so, it is because both belief and morality in Hume are inextricably bound up with the *fact of fiction*.

The narrow, epistemological reading of Hume – which, as we have already seen, Deleuze wants to forcefully break with – turns around the impressions–ideas pair. And, doubtless, the critical question 'to what impression does this idea correspond?' plays an indispensable role in the first, sceptical moment in Hume's thought, allowing us to dispense with the most flagrant of illegitimate *philosophical* assertions. It is equally clear that, without endorsing the relationship between impressions and ideas, nothing else in Hume's philosophy follows.

But, as Saul Traiger notes, it is the careless reader who would overlook the fact that Hume's pair of concepts is in fact a trinity: impressions–ideas–fictions.[1] Now, the category of fiction dominates *Empiricism and Subjectivity* from one end to the other, introducing a register of the problem irreducible, in Deleuze's view, to either simple error or philosophical hubris. There is a kind of blind dogmatism to be found in those philosophers content to merely ask for corresponding impressions. For those who have read perhaps too much Wittgenstein, it becomes possible to conclude that it is principally in the overgrown gardens of philosophy that illegitimate beliefs flower.

Hume and Deleuze both clearly reject such a thesis. It is true that the talk of philosophers can and often does lead to illegitimate beliefs, but only because the advent of belief is in general so thoroughly shot through with the excesses of the imagination. Merely discarding words like *monad*, *identity* or *soul* and adopting a posture of theoretical 'seriousness' will never be adequate to this more fundamental meaning of fiction.

Earlier I invoked the title of Francisco Goya's famous etching (a text that also, not without a certain paradox, appears in the work itself), 'The Sleep of Reason Produces Monsters', made in the very last years of the eighteenth century – Hume's century. This sentiment is in one sense the polar opposite of Hume's convictions about reason. The aberrations that arise in the mind belong, at the most basic level, to the fancy – which is to say, to the mind itself. As Walter Waxman very well puts it, the scepticism that arises from Hume's observations, both for Hume himself and his readers, is

> not a product of wild dreams or intoxicated visions (and in that sense is no nightmare) but of cold, hard reflections emblematic of reason at its soberest and most vigilant: reason determined at all costs to remain true to sound, wakeful experience and to be guided exclusively by 'principles which are permanent, irresistible, and universal'.[2]

Leibniz's monads may be among the most exotic blooms that flourish in that garden, but they share a nightshade rootstock with everything everyday, ordinary and vernacular.

The goal of this chapter will be to consider Deleuze's reflections on the problematic of fiction in Hume, the way it both circumscribes and founds human nature, and the precise limits of our means to combat it. This will mean first recapitulating certain of the analyses we have already seen, with the hope of coming to a better overall sense of Hume's system.

FICTION IN BELIEF AND MORALITY

We have already seen the double place of fiction in belief. In the first instance, beliefs are produced in the mind through the activity of the principles of association. No longer are our ideas linked together chaotically or indifferently in the fancy, and no more is the mind a simple collection. Beliefs (complex ideas) constitute views about the way things are; the mind becomes a series of habitual tendencies for future associations. In this way, the primordial indifference of the fancy has been overcome, but this is at the cost of elevating it to a new level and endowing it with a greatly expanded field of engagement. Or, as Deleuze often puts it, the principles can now be deployed in the name of the fancy. The imagination hijacks these new means, becoming an active faculty at the same time that it becomes an activated means of deception, born into the life of a double agent.

The principles of association in their primary deployment thus call for correction. This correction is the function of habit that Deleuze calls theoretical reason. Experience is essentially the repetition of cases, that is, of impressions of sensation. These impressions give rise to ideas with determinate degrees of regularity, and it is by judging the likelihood of beliefs against the backdrop of the regularity of experience that it becomes possible to assert – with a certain degree of probability – what constitutes an illegitimate belief. We know that reason here is no immutable superior faculty nor all-seeing eye of the mind, but a calm passion that habitually attaches approval or disapproval to what are likely to be legitimate and illegitimate beliefs respectively. Nevertheless, it is our means to respond to the first-order fictions of belief.

The second level of fiction arises in a range of cases where we cannot rely upon this comparative function of reason. The kinds of problems that arise can do so under a number of conditions: there may be no repetition of cases that can be used as comparative materials; the repetitions themselves may produce fictions; the principles of association (causality in particular) may even give rise on their own terms to beliefs that, because they are engendered on this basic level are too 'deep' in the structure of the mind to be addressed by it. Such examples no doubt appear opaque at the moment, and will need to be clarified in what follows. Nevertheless, fiction appears at both levels as the major problem, endemic to belief, that must be addressed. This problem, to repeat, is no mere case of error, but internal to belief, its composition and its correction: 'there are not false but illegitimate beliefs [. . .] and an illegitimate deployment of relations'.[3] The operations of the system of the understanding 'encounter fiction, and are opposed to it, without possessing the power to destroy it' (ES 85/82).

When we turn to the role of fiction in morality, Hume will present something very close to the opposite picture. We know that he conceives 'society as a positive system of invented endeavors' (ES 26/39), that both produce general interests from the materials of particular interests, and allow for their satisfaction. What is given as nature is particularity and partiality, and from these no institution naturally follows. Consequently, the entire moral world is a confection, an artifice. Moreover, we know that the various possible institutional solutions to the problems of interest find their source – like belief – in the imagination. Thus the stability of possession is only realised in the image of various imagined institutions. What Deleuze calls the determination of the institution names the necessary role of the imagination in the formation of moral reality.

In a profound sense, then, the fictions of morality are the resolution of the problems posed by fictional beliefs, even though both involve a necessary passage through the imagination. As Deleuze notes, the only real problem that attends the fictions of morality are the limitations that pertain to each general rule from its own point of view – and the solution to this problem is simply the production of more general rules.

The list of the imagination's crimes detailed in Hume's philosophy may be long, but it will be confined to crimes of belief. *Empiricism and Subjectivity* includes a scattered version of this list, which we will now briefly reconstitute. By doing this, we will become able to see, as if a result of the shadows that they cast, the capacities of human nature and their limits.

UNPHILOSOPHICAL PROBABILITY

We know that particular illegitimate beliefs are produced alongside the legitimate, but what specifically are the former, and what are their specific sources? Deleuze notes three cases in particular.

The first case is the most general. Hume describes it as 'Unphilosophical Probability' (T 1.3.13). If we understand how association functions, Hume suggests, we will be able to see each of the ways in which they can also lead us into fiction. In other words, the specific mechanism by which these illegitimate beliefs arise is easy to grasp, because it is nothing other than the mechanism that produces legitimate beliefs.

For Hume there are two obvious classes of this kind of illegitimate use of association. The first concerns the fact that, over time, the initial force conveyed by an impression to its attendant idea decays in vivacity. Consequently, we are more likely to believe what is most recent, and less likely what is further in the past. Of course, this fact itself has absolutely no bearing on the legitimacy of the belief, but it nevertheless follows from the way that beliefs are engendered. The difference between recent memories and those that have more or less faded away functions in the same way. If, Hume notes, a drunk sees his friend die from drinking too much, he will begin to reform himself immediately. As time passes, though, along with the vivacity formerly attached to the memory, he is likely to return to his previous habits (T 1.3.13.2).

So, the first kind of elementary fiction that Hume describes as unphilosophical probability arises thanks to the nature of the impression–idea relationship. The second kind concerns the principles of association more generally, and, as Deleuze will stress, involves a misconstrual of accidental features of experience – we 'confuse the essential and the accidental. In fact, the counterfeit character of beliefs always depends on an accidental characteristic' (ES 68/70). Here is Hume's very clear summary:

> In almost all kinds of causes there is a complication of circumstances, of which some are essential, and others superfluous; some are absolutely requisite to the production of the effect, and others are only conjoined by accident. Now we may observe, that when these superfluous circumstances are numerous, and remarkable, and frequently conjoined with the essential, they have such an influence on the imagination, that even in the absence of the latter they carry us on to the conception of the usual effect, and give to that conception a force and vivacity, which make it superior to the mere fictions of the fancy. (T 1.3.13.9)

Such is the source of my beliefs about my lucky shirt. The fact that I was wearing it in situations where good things happened to me is taken to be proof that it is the cause of these good things. But, in truth, the shirt was and remains (sadly) incidental to beneficent outcomes. The principles of the understanding, hypercharged by the fancy, propel me beyond what I can legitimately assert.

It bears stressing one last time that in both of these cases, the source of illegitimate beliefs is the associative apparatus itself; nothing foreign is required to intervene in order for these illusory beliefs to arise.

THE FICTIONS OF LANGUAGE AND PHILOSOPHY

The second set of fictions arises thanks to *language*. As Deleuze says, at issue is a class of *'fictitious causalities'* (ES 67/70). In straightforward sensory experience, the world that I repeatedly encounter causes impressions that in turn result in ideas, and the latter are brought together in beliefs. But repetition in experience is not the only way to repeat: 'Language, by itself, produces belief, as it substitutes observed repetition with spoken repetition, and the impression of a present object with the hearing of a specific word that allows us to conceive ideas viv- idly' (ES 67–8/70). Repetition in speech can thus produce new beliefs without any reference to experience whatsoever. The belief that all immigrants are essentially illegal – that is, mor- ally suspect – may be engendered through illegitimate uses of association in the first sense (confusing the accidental and the general), and they may also be engendered by speaking about them, but it is also the case that completely accidental expe- riences can give to language the small but sufficient materials from which ungrounded, fantastical beliefs can be completely manufactured. Thus the repetition in language of anti-immigra- tion sentiments – by media outlets, for instance, that really are morally suspect, in Hume's sense as well as others – gives rise to a veritable plague of fictions.

Finally, there is the case of *philosophy* itself, which presents us with a refined and extended case of linguistic fictions: 'The philosopher, having spoken continuously of faculties and occult qualities, ends up believing that these words "have a secret meaning, which we might discover by reflection"' (ES 68/70, quoting T 1.4.3.10). Hume devotes two sections of the *Treatise* to the fictions produced and espoused by ancient and modern philosophy respectively (T 1.4.3 and 1.4.4). And while philoso- phers are in essence guilty of the same crime as children, poets and lovers, their degree of self-deception and their arrogation of objectivity and reason lead Hume to be particularly acerbic: 'We must pardon children, because of their age; poets, because they profess to follow implicitly the suggestions of their fancy: But what excuse shall we find to justify our philosophers in so signal a weakness?' (T 1.4.3.11).

The major fictions that occupy the classical philosophers – Hume invokes without always naming them a range of pre- Socratics (Democritus is clearly recognisable at one point) and the Stoics – are crystallised in the belief in super-sensible sub- stances and super-natural capacities in thought. Here is Hume's genealogy of these beliefs, whose satirical force requires that we cite at length. After noting that these philosophers, like

Sisyphus or Tantalus, seek to grasp the very thing that they themselves define as beyond them, he writes:

> But as nature seems to have observed a kind of justice and compensation in every thing, she has not neglected philosophers more than the rest of the creation; but has reserved them a consolation amid all their disappointments and afflictions. This consolation principally consists in their invention of the words: faculty and occult quality. For it being usual, after the frequent use of terms, which are really significant and intelligible, to omit the idea, which we would express by them, and to preserve only the custom, by which we recal the idea at pleasure; so it naturally happens, that after the frequent use of terms, which are wholly insignificant and unintelligible, we fancy them to be on the same footing with the precedent, and to have a secret meaning, which we might discover by reflection. The resemblance of their appearance deceives the mind, as is usual, and makes us imagine a thorough resemblance and conformity. By this means these philosophers set themselves at ease, and arrive at last, by an illusion, at the same indifference, which the people attain by their stupidity [. . .] They need only say, that any phenomenon, which puzzles them, arises from a faculty or an occult quality, and there is an end of all dispute and enquiry upon the matter. (T 1.4.3.10)

Nietzsche's famous remark in *Beyond Good and Evil*, seems to find here its precursor:

> 'How are synthetic judgments a priori *possible*?' Kant asked himself –and what really is his answer? *'By virtue of a faculty'*: but unfortunately not in five words, but so circumstantially, venerably, and with such a display of German profundity and curlicues that people simply failed to note the comical *niaiserie allemande* involved in such an answer. People were actually beside themselves with delight over this new faculty, and the jubilation reached its climax when Kant further discovered a moral faculty in man – for at that time the Germans were still moral and not yet addicted to 'Realpolitik'. – The honeymoon of German philosophy arrived; all the young theologians of the Tubingen seminary went into the bushes – all looking for 'faculties'.[4]

The withering, humorous tone and the conclusions drawn are identical in the two philosophers. Like Nietzsche after him, Hume is absolutely hostile to all references to faculties and other mysterious explanatory entities – 'spectres in the dark' (T 1.4.4.2) – on the grounds that they explain nothing. But, again like Nietzsche, he recognises that they backhandedly reveal something very significant about those that assert them. For Hume, they reveal the structure of belief formation. For Nietzsche, the beliefs disguised in German philosophy's 'hoary and senile concepts',[5] however false, are unavoidable, 'as a foreground belief and visual evidence belonging to the perspective optics of life'.[6]

Modern philosophers, on the other hand, despite the appearance of having done away with occult qualities, truck in the same kind of fictions. In particular, Hume singles out the primary–secondary distinction: 'the new philosophy has also its ghosts. It thinks that it can recuperate reason by distinguishing primary from secondary qualities, but in the end it is no less mad than the other' (ES 83). The particular and paradoxical brand of madness of the post-Cartesian philosophers Hume is invoking here is apparent when we consider that their way of playing out the scientific legacy in order to destroy the legacy of ancient philosophy reinstates it on another level.

The modern philosophy Hume is talking about is founded on the rejection of Aristotelian physics, which demonstrates all of the features of ancient philosophy that Hume is so critical of. Descartes' claim in *The World* is as clear a formulation of this rejection:

> If you find it strange that, in explaining these elements [the basic physical constituents of reality], I do not use the qualities called 'heat,' 'cold,' 'moistness,' and 'dryness,' as the [scholastic Aristotelian] Philosophers do, I shall say that these qualities appear to me to be themselves in need of explanation. Indeed, unless I am mistaken, not only these four qualities, but all others as well, including even the forms of inanimate bodies, can be explained

without the need to suppose anything in their matter other than motion, size, shape, and arrangement of its parts.[7]

Everything in addition to these geometrical characteristics – 'colours, sounds, tastes, and smells' (T 1.4.4.6) – is considered to be merely secondary, aleatory and insignificant to science. But, Hume insists, the sceptical methodology that institutes and insists on the cut between the primary and the secondary tends to reify the former, but in a completely illegitimate way. In some deft pages (T 1.4.4.7–14), he shows that every impression of sensation we possess is composed of so-called secondary qualities, and them alone. In a nutshell, everything we experience is a secondary quality, such that, 'When we exclude these sensible qualities there remains nothing in the universe, which has such an existence' (T 1.4.4.15).

The beliefs of modern philosophy, established and circulated by a certain way of speaking about reality dubiously included under the heading of 'science', give to the ideas we gain of these experiences more reality than these same experiences warrant. It is not empirical experience that gives us the world of Cartesian geometry, but Cartesian discourse.

FIRST UNCORRECTABLE BELIEF: GOD

These three forms of fiction – non-philosophical, linguistic and philosophical – are precisely what the critical application of reason, or philosophical probability, comes to bear on, and corrects with an eye to the repetitions that arise from experience. Here, at least, 'an unforgiving calculation of probabilities can expose feigned relations or delirious fantasies that go beyond experience'.[8]

However, these are not the only fictions with which we must deal, according to Hume. The fact remains that the calculus of probability has its own limits, which is to say that there are fictions that it cannot correct. Before we discuss these fictions, we need to recall what distinguishes the association of cause and effect from resemblance and contiguity: 'we must remember that the effect of the principle of causality is not only a relation but is rather an inference according to that relation. Causality is the only relation for which there is inference' (ES 131/115). To associate ideas according to resemblance and contiguity is to compose a complex idea, a belief, and nothing else. But in the case of causality, there is also an 'if this then that' inference produced at the same time. This is why 'Hume always gives causality two related definitions: causality is the union of similar objects and also a mental inference from one object to another' (ES 65/68). This is important here because this inferential aspect of causal association, along with the 'always' that the belief itself involves, is a key part in the production of uncorrectable fictional beliefs.

The first uncorrectable fiction is the belief in God, one we briefly touched on earlier. We have already seen some of Hume's reasons for questioning religion and its philosophical armaments, but we need to distinguish these from the belief in God itself. Even once natural and revealed religion are subjected to rigorous rational critique and to social moderation (and ultimately amelioration), the belief in God may still persist.

We know that it is fruitless to think we could ever know anything about the origins or nature of the principles of human nature – all belief originally arises from impressions, and we have no impressions of the principles. Our only access is to their effects, which can always be seen to be in play. We can nevertheless think about the principles; more precisely, we ask ourselves what caused the principles themselves. And it is here that a belief in God arises:

> We cannot make use of the principles of association to know the world as an effect of divine activity, and even less to know God as the cause of the world; but we can always think of God negatively, *as the cause of the principles*. (ES 78/77; my emphasis)

To be more precise yet again, the idea of God is the idea of an '*originary unity of origin and qualification*' (ES 78/77), of nature and human nature.

91

Note the role played here by causal association, now being deployed completely outside of its legitimate extension. It allows us to explain how it is that our experience of the world and the world itself fit together, but this is an explanation that can be neither proven nor disproven. Even to describe it as illegitimate can only have a limited sense. Beliefs that cannot be accounted for in terms of their basic components (ideas, and hence impressions) are always illegitimate, but beyond asserting this we can say nothing critical about it. The belief in God thus lies beyond our capacity to correct it, rationally or institutionally, and it is in this sense that 'religion is justified, but only in its very special situation, outside culture and outside true knowledge' (ES 77/77).

SECOND UNCORRECTABLE BELIEF: THE WORLD

Above, I made the following statement: *In straightforward sensory experience, the world that I repeatedly encounter causes impressions that in turn result in ideas, and the latter are brought together in beliefs.* This way of phrasing the point is in fact problematic, given the way that it uses the idea of the world.

Belief in the existence of the world is clearly illegitimate. We never encounter it in experience, which is to say that we can never point to the impressions to which the belief corresponds. However, if we try to undermine it with the critical apparatus of reason, we confront an insuperable problem. The probabilistic correction of beliefs relies upon the repetition of objects in experience. But – precisely – there is only *one* world and it is omnipresent. We do not experience any repetition here, but simply an absolute, irreducible and singular permanence. As Deleuze writes, 'The world as such is essentially the Unique' (ES 75/75). At the same time, the world is not an object. Belief in the existence of the world clearly differs from the belief in the existence of a love letter surreptitiously hidden in one's coat pocket. Rather than being one thing, the world is the supposed

92

general ontological background in which other objects come into relation – 'In other words, there are no physical objects or objects of repetition except in the world' (ES 75/75).

Deleuze summarises this situation very well in the following passage:

> The excessive rules of knowledge openly contradict the principles of association; to correct them amounts to denouncing their fiction. A distinct and continuous world is, from the point of view of the principles, the general residue of this fiction, being situated at a level that makes it impossible to be corrected. (ES 149/131)

The world is not an object of possible experience, but an unavoidable precipitate of the rules that make experience possible. Every time we conceive or reason about discrete objects and their interactions, we imply the existence of the world qua 'horizon which every object presupposes' (ES 81/80).

THIRD UNCORRECTABLE BELIEF: OBJECTHOOD

The third and final uncorrectable belief no doubt appears trivial in light of the previous two, namely the belief in distinct objects, and in their persistence over time.[9] The unobjectionable character of objects is merely apparent, though, for in fact these beliefs constitute the delirious core of human experience. The ubiquity and significance of the belief in objects is a swarm of fictions, at once the ground of all reasoning concerning causation and the most far-reaching perversion of causal association itself.

The beliefs that compose the idea of objecthood involve two different registers of fiction. The first of these is the belief in the persistence of objects, that is, the continuity of their existence. The 'constancy and resemblance of appearances cause the imagination to attribute to similar appearances the identity of an invariable object' (ES 80/79). The obvious fictional character of this belief – given that we only ever possess discrete impressions – is nevertheless particularly easy to assent to, an ease that founds all assertions about things in the world. This is to say that 'the imagination [. . .] feigns continuous existence in order to overcome the opposition between the identity of resembling perceptions and the discontinuity of appearances' (ES 80/79). Without this fabulation of continuity, there could be no coherent experience whatsoever. This is why Deleuze notes that not only is 'the fiction of continuity incorrigible, it cannot and should not be corrected' (ES 81/79).

The second component is independence, the belief that experience is the result of our encounter with objects as they exist in themselves. This is already what we have seen in the earlier brief discussion of the history of philosophy. Both the ancient category of substances and the modern thesis of primary qualities assert the independent existence of a bedrock of things to which accidents or secondary qualities are attached. Now, these beliefs result from an illegitimate deployment of causal association. Its proper use is to associate ideas, but whenever we conceive of an object as the cause of my impressions of it, we use it to bind together an object and an impression. Once again, though, we are not in a position to correct this belief. Indeed, this belief is as essential as continuity, because without it the very notion of experience itself is evacuated of meaning – without the belief in objects as the cause of what I experience, all is hallucinatory.

A striking and paradoxical situation is thus exposed: the facts of experience themselves contradict the possibility of justified belief. The true tension here lies not between things and experience, but between the fictionalising capacity of the imagination and the regulative function of the principles of association, between the fancy and the system of the understanding, between '*the imagination and the principles of reason*' (ES 84/82).

FICTION AS A PRINCIPLE OF HUMAN NATURE

On the one hand, then, 'continuity and distinctness are outright fictions and illusions of the imagination, since they revolve around, and designate that which, by definition, is not offered to any possible experience' (ES 80/78–9). But on the other, without these fictions, it would be impossible to form any beliefs whatsoever. If we recall the examples we have discussed so far – billiards, backgammon and shirts, property ownership, government and commerce – it is easy to see that, without the supposition of a unity of objects of experience, they come entirely undone.

The choice appears to be between fictional beliefs and no beliefs at all – *'between contradiction and nothingness'* (ES 87/83) – but in truth we do not have this choice. We are led therefore to assert that fiction, far from being a contingent and occasional by-product of belief, is necessary and ubiquitous, and that it cannot be corrected. But this leads to the conclusion that fiction itself is *'a principle of human nature'* (ES 82/80). In Deleuze's view, 'The most important point is to be found here.' He continues, writing that

> The entire sense of the principles of human nature is to transform the *multiplicity* of ideas which constitute the mind into a *system*, that is, a system of knowledge and of its objects. But for a system to exist, it is not enough to have ideas associated in the mind [. . .] We must give the object of the idea an existence which does not depend on the senses. (ES 82/80)

The system of the understanding can never by itself produce this necessary but fabulous certitude. This is the true meaning of what Deleuze calls the third, final act of belief. The idea of God is the object of possible intellectual engagement, and that of the world a residue of all such engagement. But the belief in the persistence of objects is the foundation of all other beliefs, the phantasmatic presupposition of the system of the understanding itself. The depths of thought are indeed mad; the immense, distorted shadow play cast by our everyday lives and thoughts, a carnival parade of fictional entities and obscure powers worthy of Roussel, Lovecraft or Borges.

PURPOSIVENESS

We noted earlier that the idea of God may be invoked whenever we enquire after the origin of the principles. As an idea, it is completely vacuous. We can always produce it, but never legitimately give it any particular content. There are of course ways of providing this content, but not without contravening the rule of experience. For instance, in the first *Enquiry*, Hume suggests that 'The idea of God, as meaning an infinitely intelligent, wise, and good Being, arises from reflecting on the operations of our own mind, and augmenting, without limit, those qualities of goodness and wisdom' (EHU 2.6).

At the formal level, as Deleuze notes, the idea of God in the negative sense constitutes a belief in the '*originary unity of origin and qualification*' (ES 78/77), the primordial harmony of nature itself and the human nature that apprehends it. This thread is the one that Deleuze will once more pick up in the second half of *Empiricism and Subjectivity*, even going so far as to title the conclusion of the book with the term he gives this topic: 'purposiveness'.

In the English translation of *Empiricism and Subjectivity*, 'purposiveness' renders Deleuze's *la finalité*. While this may seem like an odd choice, and while 'finality' is certainly both more elegant and more svelte, it correctly reflects the use of its cognate 'purpose' in 'the posthumous *Dialogues concerning Natural Religion*, which may be [Hume's] masterpiece'.[10] Also involved, as Christian Kerslake notes, is a passing use of the notion of 'pre-established harmony' (EHU 5.21), in the first *Enquiry*.[11] It is also true though that what Deleuze says here is much more reminiscent of the concept of *Zweckmäßigkeit* advanced by Kant in the third *Critique*. We will return to all of these points later in the book.

Deleuze's reflections on this concept are threaded throughout *Empiricism and Subjectivity*, but begin to be explicitly addressed in relation to the subordination of association and belief to morality and invention. He recalls a point we have already seen (in terms we will examine in the next chapter), namely that 'The association of ideas does not define a knowing subject, but to the contrary a set of possible means for a practical subject for whom all real ends belong to the passional, moral, political, and economic order' (ES 120/138). What this presupposes is that the order of belief and the order of morality form a certain natural whole, or exhibit a natural fittingness. And this is precisely what is meant here by *purposiveness*: not an orientation towards a completion, but an original, originary harmony of purpose. This is why Deleuze immediately continues by writing that 'this subordination of association to the passions already manifests within human nature a kind of secondary purposiveness, which prepares us for the problem of primary purposiveness, that is, for the problem of the agreement between human nature and nature' (ES 138/121).

We have already seen that the secondary or 'intentional' (ES 150/132) purposiveness that characterises the relationship between morality and belief is a function of the practical neutrality of belief and the practical remedy morality provides to belief's natural excesses. That is, secondary purposiveness is grounded in the absolute primacy of the moral order. But primary purposiveness – Deleuze almost always simply calls it purposiveness – also involves two non-symmetrical halves, nature and human nature: 'We call purposiveness this agreement between intentional finality and nature' (ES 152/133).

On the one hand, and again like the belief in object permanence, a belief in purposiveness appears necessary if we are to give any stock to any other belief. To be more precise, we must believe in both the fittingness of our experience to what we experience and the fact that the former conforms to the latter and not the other way around: 'At this point, Hume's philosophy reaches its ultimate point: Nature conforms to being. Human nature conforms to nature' (ES 152/133). But on the other hand, this is clearly an illegitimate belief, even the apotheosis of such beliefs. It 'can only be thought; and it is undoubtedly the weakest and emptiest of thoughts' (ES 152/133).

Now, as in the case of secondary purposiveness, there is a way to come to grips with the deadlock between the two halves, one found in the order not of moral but of *philosophical* practice, and one that plays a central role in Deleuze's definition of empiricism, as we will see. For now, we need only notice the way in which the problem itself shows theoretical reason at its furthest extension. The idea of a natural fit between nature and human nature presents us with nothing less than the fundamental structure of experience. But at the very same time it is an idea that can never be justified, proven or even tested. It glimmers with a now familiar mad sheen.

We might therefore consider adding purposiveness to the list of God, the object and the world, each of which names an indissoluble fiction involved in the production of belief in the mind. But is it true to characterise it as a fictional belief? In a sense – and Deleuze means nothing when he says that the thought of purposiveness is the emptiest thought – it presents the understanding with the very form of all fictional belief. But *for precisely this same reason*, purposiveness reveals the outline of human nature itself. In the powerless and empty thought we glimpse the power and nascent content of human nature.

INDIFFERENCE, MADNESS, DELIRIUM

Deleuze concludes the middle chapter of *Empiricism and Subjectivity*, 'God and the World', with a remarkable summary of the relationship between subjectivity and fiction, identifying what he calls the 'three critical states of the mind' (ES 88/84). This summary issues from 'the point of view of philosophy' (ES 86/83), that is, the vantage point offered by reason, whose interest in qualifying beliefs is confronted with its opposite.

The first critical state is what Deleuze calls '*[i]ndifference and fancy*', which are 'the situations proper to the mind, independent of the external principles which fix it by associating its ideas' (ES 87/83). We have already insisted on the fact that the imagination in its guise as fancy is not a developmental stage slowly overcome or consumed (or 'decimated', to use Deleuze's peculiar word), but a persistent state or level in the organisation of the mind, akin to the unconscious.

The second critical state is what Deleuze calls *madness* (*démence*), which he defines as 'the contradiction in the mind between these principles which affect it and the fiction which it affirms as a principle' (ES 88/84). We saw that this holds particularly true in the belief in the persistence of objects, where this outright fiction appears not as an exception to the law-like operation of the understanding but its necessary presupposition.

Finally, there is *delirium*, 'the system of fictional reconciliations between principles and fiction' (ES 88/84), and here our focus shifts from the rift at the heart of association to the powerlessness of theoretical reason to bridge it. We know that all the probabilistic correction of beliefs can do is determine the comparative likelihood that these beliefs are legitimate. But legitimacy is determined by the coherence of a given belief with the ongoing course of experience, and this latter is demented, a crazed ad hoc bricolage. Consequently, reason is profoundly incapable of addressing fictional beliefs. Its warrant to correct is founded on the madness of thought; left to its own devices, it can only guarantee that certainty 'is compromised and lost' (ES 88/84).

In sum, the system of the understanding is 'a mad delirium' (ES 87/83).

But as deranged as it has revealed itself to be, we already know what will charge its indifference with purpose, and rein in its madness: 'the entire domain of general rules and beliefs' (ES 89/84):

This domain is the middle and temperate region, where the contradiction between human nature and the imagination already exists, and always subsists, but this contradiction is regulated by possible corrections and resolved through practice. In short there is no science or life except at the level of general rules and beliefs. (ES 89/84)

Here, at the heart of Hume's thought, we encounter once again the double role of fiction in the 'fictional reconciliations between principles and fiction' (ES 88/84). In the understanding, everything unravels along this seam, but in morality, the sphere of practice and invention, fictional reconciliations constitute a real and moderating influence on the understanding. Practical reason is entirely as delirious as the understanding, but now in the service of a positive construction rather than an empty and endless spiral in the void.

In one respect, to arrive at this point is to arrive at the terminus of Deleuze's recapitulation of Hume's philosophy in *Empiricism and Subjectivity*. We have seen how the passage from the indifference of the imagination as fancy to its ongoing determination in social life, complex though it may be, comes about. This is to mark out the spherical space of practical reason, with its perpetually rewoven moral whole. Parallel to this, we have seen theoretical reason at its furthest extension and greatest vacuity in the thought of finality – the gesture reason makes across an abyss it can never traverse.

But it would be equally fair to say that everything we have seen so far remains preparatory. For we have yet to examine either of the concepts that form the title of Deleuze's book in any more than scant depth. What, in fact, is the subject in Hume? And in what way does empiricism give us particular resources to define it?

NOTES

1. Saul Traiger, 'Impressions, Ideas, and Fictions', *Hume Studies* 13:2 (1987), 381–99.
2. Walter Waxman, *Hume's Theory of Consciousness* (Cambridge: Cambridge University Press, 1994), 271, quoting T 1.4.4.1. On the seriousness of the sceptical problem for Hume as a philosopher, see the important, corrective discussion in Terence Penelhum, 'Hume's Moral Psychology', in *The Cambridge Companion to Hume*, ed. David Fate Norton (Cambridge: Cambridge University Press, 1993), 117–20.

3. Gilles Deleuze, 'Hume', in *Desert Islands and Other Texts*, ed. David Lapoujade, trans. Michael Taormina (New York: Semiotext(e), 2004), 165.

4. Friedrich Nietzsche, 'On the Prejudices of the Philosophers', §11, in *Beyond Good and Evil*, in *Basic Writings of Nietzsche*, ed. and trans. Walter Kaufmann (New York: The Modern Library, 1992).

5. Nietzsche, 'On the Prejudices of the Philosophers', §11.

6. Nietzsche, 'On the Prejudices of the Philosophers', §11.

7. René Descartes, *The World and Other Writings*, ed. and trans. Stephen Gaukroger (Cambridge: Cambridge University Press, 1998), 18.

8. Deleuze, 'Hume', 165.

9. In his later summary of Hume's philosophy, Deleuze drops the reference to objects, and even more clearly aligns his reading with the framework of Kantianism: 'the illegitimate beliefs in the World, the Self, and God appear as the horizon of every possible legitimate belief, or as the lowest degree of belief' (Deleuze, 'Hume', 166). Since our goal is to explicate *Empiricism and Subjectivity*, this point can be left aside here, except to note that Deleuze does discuss the fiction of the self (though in the context of his account of subjectivity rather than illegitimate belief) there, and to note that we will discuss the pronounced Kantian character of Deleuze's Hume in the final chapter here.

10. Deleuze, 'Hume', 166.

11. Christian Kerslake, *Immanence and the Vertigo of Philosophy: From Kant to Deleuze* (Edinburgh: Edinburgh University Press, 2009), 101–2.

5

Subjectivity

At the end of the previous chapter, I suggested that we had not yet broached the topic of subjectivity as Deleuze accounts for it in *Empiricism and Subjectivity*. This is not quite true. In fact, the category of the subject has already appeared in three forms.

It first appeared as a fiction entertained by certain philosophers, one that can be quickly undermined by attending to what is actually found in the mind. Introspecting, I do not find anything that deserves the name 'self', but only

> a bundle or collection of different perceptions, which succeed each other with an inconceivable rapidity, and are in a perpetual flux and movement [. . .] The mind is a kind of theatre, where several perceptions successively make their appearance; pass, repass, glide away, and mingle in an infinite variety of postures and situations. (T 1.4.6.4)

This is, of course, a devastating critique for any theory of the self that conceives it as a substance that we ought to be able to directly intuit. However, we have also seen that Hume himself makes use of the concept of self in his definition of the passions of pride and humility:

> It is evident, that pride and humility, though directly contrary, have yet the same OBJECT. This object is self, or that succession

of related ideas and impressions, of which we have an intimate memory and consciousness. Here the view always fixes when we are actuated by either of these passions. According as our idea of ourself is more or less advantageous, we feel either of those opposite affections, and are elated by pride, or dejected with humility. Whatever other objects may be comprehended by the mind, they are always considered with a view to ourselves; otherwise they would never be able either to excite these passions, or produce the smallest encrease or diminution of them. (T 2.1.2.2)

Taken together, these passages seem to constitute a contradiction. As Norman Kemp Smith puts it,

> Why is it that in Book I of the *Treatise* the existence of an impression of the self is explicitly denied, while yet his theory of the 'indirect' passions, propounded at length in Book II, is made to rest on the assumption that we do in fact experience an impression of the self, and that this impression is ever-present to us?[1]

The equivalence Hume draws between 'self' and 'that succession of related ideas and impressions, of which we have an intimate memory and consciousness' is what allows him to avoid this charge of self-contradiction. What I *feel* to be myself is not some self-identical non-physical substance like the Cartesian *cogito* – which, in any case, would require more than sensation to guarantee – but a set of habitually associated ideas and their concomitant impressions.

Pursuing the direction indicated by this latter conception of self will bring us closer to the central claim advanced in Deleuze's reading of Hume. None of these uses of the concept of self, though – as fiction, as 'bundle', as 'succession of related ideas and impressions' – is precisely what he wishes to designate by the term 'subjectivity'. Let us also note very clearly the fact that the term 'subjectivity' does not appear in Hume's philosophy – it is not even true, as Deleuze suggests, that it is 'very rarely used by Hume'.[2] It would be no exaggeration to claim then that Deleuze's greatest gambit in *Empiricism and Subjectivity* is his claim that there is a coherent account of subjectivity in Hume that Hume never makes explicit under this name, even if it is one that complements and extends the minimal uses of the term 'self' we have just seen.[3]

HUME'S QUESTION

The seam that runs through *Empiricism and Subjectivity* from beginning to end can be called 'Hume's question'. Deleuze first presents it in this form: 'the question which will preoccupy Hume is this: *how does the mind become human nature?*' (ES 22). But, starting on the same page, he will begin to further iterate its formulation, threading it through many of the major concepts in Hume's philosophy:

how does a collection become a system? (ES 2/22)

Then again the question may be: *how does the mind become a subject?* How does the imagination become a faculty? (ES 2/23)

how can a subject that transcends the given be constituted in the given? (ES 91–2/86)

When is the subject the product of the principles of human nature? (ES 123/109)

We know that the question 'how is the subject constituted within the given?' means 'how does the imagination become a faculty?' (ES 124/110; cf. 136/119)[4]

So the question no longer concerns the mechanisms of belief and general interest, but the nature of the subject whose beliefs and interests are in question. The hinge around which both turn is the notion of *transcendence*. Even though their mechanisms differ, both morality and belief involve transcendence: beliefs transcend the given ('the sun will rise tomorrow'), institutions transcend the particularities of my interests.

At the same time, the essence of subjectivity will be to transcend the collection of ideas in the mind as such: 'The only content we can give to the idea of subjectivity is that of mediation and transcendence' (ES 90/85). The entire problem then becomes one of defining the nature of the movement of transcendence that will take the mind from passive receptivity to active transcendence. That is, 'The subject is defined by the movement through which it is developed' (ES 90/85).

TWO NON-HUMEAN NON-ANSWERS

Before we turn to the Humean answer, we should briefly consider the two non-Humean alternatives that Deleuze tables by way of comparison – two non-Humean answers to 'Hume's question'.

The first of these, the answer provided by what Deleuze designates the psychology of the mind, we have already briefly touched on. It is both the most straightforward alternative but also the easiest to reject for reasons we have also already seen. The psychology of the mind asserts that the consistency of the mind is provided by a real and primary subsistent self. In turn, the passage from collection to system is effected by this self, which also means that the self is not affected by this passage.

This approach is categorically undermined by Hume's sceptical introspector. There is no evidence within experience that any such subject exists: 'never can catch myself at any time without a perception, and never can observe any thing but the perception' (T 1.4.6.3). Or, put another way, 'The psychology of the mind is impossible, unable to be constituted, being unable to find in its object the required constancy or universality' (ES 1/21). What constitutes subjective experience does not present us with what we would need to advance the thesis of the subsistent self.

The second answer is Kant's, and constitutes a much more subtle and powerful challenge to Hume, precisely because Kant completely accepts the critique of the psychology of the mind, and recognises the impossibility of obtaining any true beliefs about the existence of the self as if it were an object of experience: 'Inner sense, by means of which the mind intuits itself, or its inner state, gives, to be sure, no intuition of the soul itself, as an object.'[5]

Here is the passage in which Deleuze marks out the key divergence between Kant and Hume:

> The question of empiricism, 'how does the subject constitute itself within the given?', suggests that we distinguish two things: on one hand, that the necessary recourse to principles for the understanding of subjectivity is affirmed; but on the other, that the agreement between principles and the given within which the principles constitute the subject is given up. The principles of experience are not principles for the objects of experience, they do not guarantee the reproduction of objects within experience. (ES 136/119)

For both Hume and Kant, we have the given on the one hand, and certain principles on the other, that together constitute objects of experience – complex ideas for Hume, representations for Kant. But for Kant, as Deleuze notes, the principles that constitute representations are also the principles that constitute the possibility of the subjective experience of these representations. As a famous line from the first *Critique* has it, 'The *a priori* conditions of a possible experience in general are at the same time conditions of the possibility of objects of experience.'[6]

In other words, the split between Hume and Kant concerns the location of the split between the object and the operation of the principles. For Hume, what is given is fundamentally just an indifferently ordered collection of ideas, in itself subject to no principle (indeed, insubordinate in its being). For Kant, the given is already phenomenal, structured by the forms of intuition and the categories of the understanding. The radical dualism between the given and subjectivity that characterises all empiricism for Deleuze (more on this in the next chapter) is therefore entirely absent for Kant.

107

In the first quotation above, Deleuze alludes to the problem of reproduction, that is, repetition – indeed, before the passage I cited, Deleuze himself cites a long text that falls under the heading 'On the synthesis of reproduction in the imagination'.[7] While Kant does not mention Hume's name here, the problem he raises is certainly a problem for accounts like Hume's. His claim amounts to this: if my only means for establishing that I was experiencing 'the same thing' is habitual and experiential, then no knowledge would ever be possible. Famously, Kant writes that

> If cinnabar were now red, now black, now light, now heavy, If a human being were now changed into this animal shape, now into that one, If on the longest day the land were covered now with fruits, now with ice and snow, then my empirical imagination would never even get the opportunity to think of heavy cinnabar on the occasion of the representation of the color red; or if a certain word were attributed now to this thing, now to that, or if one and the same thing were sometimes called this, sometimes that, without the governance of a certain rule to which the appearances are already subjected in themselves, then no empirical synthesis of reproduction could take, place.[8]

This is a problem we have already encountered when we discussed the limits of belief and the limited corrective capacities of theoretical reason. In both Hume and Kant, there is a recognition of the potentially catastrophic power of repetition, which is to say its unrestricted productive capacity. For the Kant of the first *Critique*, this power is abjured by having the objects of experience produced within the framework of subjectivity as such. Reiteration thus always takes place in a context that provides, a priori, a means for re-cognition. For Hume, as we know, there is no absolute way to resolve the threat of lawless repetition. It can only be mollified by being subordinated to the practical ends of the moral world.

Deleuze again cites precisely this passage from the first *Critique* in *Kant's Critical Philosophy*, and, once again, it provides him with an opportunity to contrast Kantian and Humean philosophy in even clearer terms than we find in *Empiricism and Subjectivity*:

> We can see the point where Kant breaks with Hume. Hume had clearly seen that knowledge implied subjective principles, by means of which we go beyond the given. But these principles seemed to him merely principles of *human nature*, psychological principles of association concerning our own representations. Kant transforms the problem: that which is presented to us in such a way as to form a Nature must necessarily obey principles of the same kind (or rather, the *same principles*) as those which govern the course of our representations.[9]

In any case, both of these answers to 'Hume's question' appear to Deleuze as a species of non-answer, a way of avoiding the question of the constitution of the subject. Let us recall that, for Deleuze, we must define the subject in terms of 'the movement through which it is developed' (ES 85). But both the Kantian and psychologistic accounts presuppose the subject – or, better, they both refuse the Humean way of framing the problem, since for them there is no developmental movement constitutive of the subject itself. Thus 'Hume's merit lies in the singling out of this empirical problem in its pure state and its separation from the transcendental and the psychological' (ES 92/87).

FROM SENSATION TO REFLECTION

The narrow epistemological reading of Hume in the Kantian tradition that we began the book by sidestepping places enormous weight on the opposition between impressions and ideas, or, to be more precise, impressions of *sensation* and ideas. If this approach, this set of concepts, is pursued without reference to any other, we arrive at the sceptical conclusion that the term 'subject' has no justifiable referent.

Deleuze's whole account of the Humean subject turns around a distinction, key in Hume and articulated very early in the *Treatise*, that this opposition puts to one side: the distinction between impressions of sensation and impressions of reflection. Here is Deleuze's starting point: 'The impressions of sensation are only the origin of the mind; as for the impressions of reflection, they are the qualification of the mind and the effect of principles in it' (ES 15/31). The sceptical reading of Hume's project, and the priority granted to the impression–idea pair are mutually presupposed and, at least in the way that they are engaged with, tend towards the exclusion of the much more important effects of the principles constituted through reflection.

Here is how Hume presents the two kinds of impressions very early in the *Treatise*:

> Impressions may be divided into two kinds, those Of SENSATION and those of REFLEXION. The first kind arises in the soul originally, from unknown causes. The second is derived in a great measure from our ideas, and that in the following order. An impression first strikes upon the senses, and makes us perceive heat or cold, thirst or hunger, pleasure or pain of some kind or other. Of this impression there is a copy taken by the mind, which remains after the impression ceases; and this we call an idea. This idea of pleasure or pain, when it returns upon the soul, produces the new impressions of desire and aversion, hope and fear, which may properly be called impressions of reflexion, because derived from it. (T 1.1.2.1)

We can therefore add that the impression–idea distinction, as it is deployed in the epistemological reading of Hume, is one-sided in a further respect (in addition, that is, to the addition of fictions to the list): it only presents the activity of the principles of human nature from a very limited point of view. And the price to be paid for this limited point of view, for Deleuze, is nothing other than the loss of subjectivity *tout court*. How so?

In the passage from the *Treatise* cited above, the principles of human nature are not mentioned. It is by introducing them to the analysis that we finally attain the beachhead of the concept of subjectivity. Here is Deleuze:

We must start from the pure impression and begin with principles. Principles, Hume says, act inside the mind. But what is their
action? The answer is unambiguous: the effect of the principle is
always an impression of reflection. Subjectivity is then an impression of reflection and nothing else. (ES 127/113)

Impressions of sensation give rise to ideas, as their pale images
or copies in the mind, and these subsist after the impression
itself has faded. In the wake of this process, certain of these
ideas are replayed in the mind – but why these ideas and not
others? We already know that the answer is the principles of
human nature. First of all, then, the principles function in a
selective fashion. The passage from a collection to a system
necessarily has this as its first moment, but this cannot be all,
because this selective function does not explain why the result
of the initial selection returns again in the mind, engendering
then impressions of reflection – the genuine creations of the
mind itself. Thus, 'The role of principles in general is both to
designate impressions of sensation and, based upon them, to
produce an impression of reflection' (ES 129/114).[10] To flesh
this out this double process, Deleuze presents the example of
one of the principles of association:

the principle of resemblance designates certain ideas that are similar, and makes it possible to group them together under the same
name. Based on this name and in conjunction with a certain idea
taken from the group – for example, a particular idea awakened
by the name – the principle produces a habit, a strength, and a
power to evoke any other particular idea of the same group; it
produces an impression of reflection. (ES 129/114)

Deleuze mentions the absolutely central point here: 'the principle
produces a habit'. The true products of the principles of association are not complex ideas, just as the true products of general
rules are not socialised values. This is actually a quite partial
and, by itself, misleading perspective on the subject in Hume. In
both cases, *what is produced is subjectivity*, a habitual, inventive

subject, and the beliefs and general rules that follow are the fruit of subjectivity, not the subject itself.

> From what is given, I infer the existence of that which is not given: I believe. Caesar is dead, Rome did exist, the sun will rise, and bread is nourishing. At the same time and through the same operation, while transcending the given, I judge and posit myself as subject. I affirm more than I know. Therefore, the problem of truth must be presented and stated as the critical problem of subjectivity itself. (ES 90/85–6)

While we will elaborate on this point at length in what follows, this is the essence of Humean subjectivity: an activated system of habitual tendencies. The passage from collection to system is therefore not at all a passage from simple to complex ideas, but from the perceptions in the mind to a subject that habitually organises these perceptions. 'The mind, having become nature, becomes *tendency*' (ES 7/23). Or, in perhaps his clearest summary of the point, Deleuze asks:

> what do we mean when we speak of the subject? We mean that the imagination, having been a collection, becomes now a faculty; the distributed collection becomes now a system. The given is reprised in a movement that transcends it. The mind becomes human nature. The subject invents and believes; *it is synthesis, a synthesis of the mind.* (ES 100/92)

Let me note in passing that while I have so far more or less used 'self' and 'subject' interchangeably, as Deleuze himself sometimes does, we can now be more precise. The *subject* will be defined as the agent of belief and institutional invention, itself engendered through reflection. The *self* will be the subject, plus the perceptions possessed by the subject, both collection and system, both 'mind and subject' (ES 15/31).

SUBJECTIVITY AND QUALIFICATION

There is a second way in which Deleuze also presents the same definition of subjectivity, one that bears a corrective function.

If we conceive of the subject in the terms we have just seen, it is possible to incorrectly grasp the principles as formal rules proper to the mind as such, that is, as a level of structure that exists (or insists) in the mind in excess of both collection and system. But as we have seen, the fundamental characteristic of the principles of human nature is that we only know them by their effects. We infer their existence from the ubiquity of their effects, and we can insist on their necessity only because without them there would be no order to the mind at all: 'Were ideas entirely loose and unconnected, chance alone would join them' (T 1.1.4.1). 'If cinnabar were now red, now black, now light, now heavy . . .'.[11]

What are the effects in which we recognise the principles at work? In short, they *qualify* certain perceptions: her angry email response was unwarranted, the white ball caused the red ball to move, this court ruling is unjust. As Hume puts it at the very start of the *Treatise*, the principles of human nature are the 'original qualities of human nature' (T Introduction 8). Or in Deleuze's equally brief phrase, 'human nature is qualificatory' (ES 112/101). So the key distinction, at least from this point of view, is not between the principles and the collection onto which they come to bear, but between the ideas that are unqualified by the principles and those that are. Consequently, as Deleuze notes, 'The proper role of the impressions of reflection, being effects of the principles, is to *qualify* in various ways the mind as subject' (ES 13/30). A well-known moment from the English preface to *Empiricism and Subjectivity* puts the point like this:

> We start with atomic parts, but these atomic parts have transitions, passages, 'tendencies,' which circulate from one to another. These tendencies give rise to *habits*. Isn't this the answer to the question 'what are we?' We are habits, nothing but habits – the habit of saying 'I.' (ES x)

Now, not only does subjectivity arise through this qualification of ideas, but once so qualified it takes up and elaborates this activity on its own. The mind, having become human nature, continues along the paths established for it by the principles:

> what does the mind do after becoming subject? It '*advises* certain ideas rather than others.' 'To transcend' means exactly this. The mind is animated when the principles fix it, as they establish relations between ideas; it is animated when they activate it, in the sense that they give to the vividness of impressions certain laws of communication, distribution, and allotment. In fact, *a relation between two ideas is also the quality by means of which an impression communicates to that idea something of its vividness.* (ES 144/127)[12]

It is this further specification that allows us to really get at what distinguishes Hume from Kant. Before, we saw that the given in Kant is always subordinated to the activity of principles (ultimately, these are just the machinery of the transcendental subject itself). The given is always already phenomena, unlike in Hume, where the given is given to us without presupposing the activity of a set of principles. But now we see the real effect of the principles for Hume is to constitute not mental content, but a subject who produces mental content. For Kant, both experience and what is experienced presuppose (the same) principles; for Hume, only the subject requires such a presupposition.

We also see, consequently, just how damaging it is to read Hume in terms of the familiar impression–idea pair, cast in an epistemological register. If we suppress the key role played by the subject in Hume's philosophy, the Kantian invocation of the transcendental subject appears as an inevitable and fatal critique and corrective. But since a specifically *empiricist* formulation of the subject presupposed by all beliefs can be found, we instead find ourselves before two points of view that diverge on a key point.

A PROCESSUAL SUBJECTIVITY

But to the punctual production of beliefs and institutions, and the production of the believing and inventing subject, we can add, finally, a third accent or facet of the analysis. Consider the following passage that appears near the end of Hume's discussion of the passions in the *Treatise*:

> Now if we consider the human mind, we shall find, that with regard to the passions, it is not the nature of a wind-instrument of music, which in running over all the notes immediately loses the sound after the breath ceases; but rather resembles a string-instrument, where after each stroke the vibrations still retain some sound, which gradually and insensibly decays. The imagination is extreme quick and agile; but the passions are slow and restive: For which reason, when any object is presented, that affords a variety of views to the one, and emotions to the other; though the fancy may change its views with great celerity; each stroke will not produce a clear and distinct note of passion, but the one passion will always be mixt and confounded with the other. (T 2.3.9.12)

Deleuze cites the first part of this passage in *Empiricism and Subjectivity*, and fragments of it in the later encyclopaedia piece on Hume,[13] in order to illustrate the process by which the subject is constituted. Elsewhere, as we have seen, he tends to speak of a simple 'before' and 'after', as if a single act were in question. The 'resonance' (ES 150/132) that the metaphor captures conveys very well the gradual way in which the subject is constituted in the mind. Impressions of reflection are akin to the rich echoes produced in the body of the cello when a bow passes across its strings, and each note that is played adds further depth and amplitude to the sound. The selective activity of the principles, it is true, functions on a case-by-case basis, but in their secondary, constitutive role, they gradually integrate and enlarge the scope of subjectivity, qua inventor and believer.

The key point is thus that

> To the extent that the principles sink their effect into the depths of the mind, the subject, which is this very effect, becomes more and more active, and less and less passive. It was passive in the beginning, it is active in the end [. . .] To speak like Bergson, let us say

115

that the subject is an imprint, or an impression, left by principles, that it progressively turns into a machine capable of using this impression. (ES 127/112–13)

Now, there is a danger in this last characterisation that we might misconstrue what Deleuze and Hume mean by 'active', and take it to mean that a radically free intellect is – somehow – born from a passive set of indifferently collated perceptions (ideas and impressions). The kind of activity of the mind that is engendered through the activity of the principles of human nature is that not of a free agent, but of a system of habits. In turn, the passivity that is overcome is not the passivity *of* the subject, since at this level of the analysis there is no subject. Here, the thematic of transcendence provides a useful corrective. The subject is defined as what transcends the given, but this transcendence is not itself a power or capacity of the subject but 'an empirical fact' (ES 125/111) observable because there is subjectivity.

In the first instance, we cannot but assert the mind's passivity: 'the mind cannot be activated by the principles of nature without remaining passive. It only suffers the effects' (ES 7/26). It is also true that this passive moment of the mind subsists in subjectivity, since we never have any power over the principles of human nature nor the source of the impressions of sensation. The active subject is simply the complex set of means, engendered in the subject as we have just seen, for going beyond the passivity proper to the mind.

Now in fact this particular text of Hume's does not lend itself to Deleuze's purposes quite as well as he indicates, since the point for Hume is that the complex resonance of the string instrument decays over time. But Deleuze's point is the opposite one: that as the principles of human nature play upon the mind, the symphony of subjectivity becomes ever richer, augmented at each turn. Nonetheless, we can see why the secondary, constitutive and creative effect of the principles is well expressed through a reference to music.

And there is another peculiarity – an irony even – in the use of this metaphor, for in fact Deleuze (in the French text of *Empiricism and Subjectivity*) does not refer to Hume's 'string-instrument', but to a percussion instrument. The source of the confusion is not Deleuze, but rather the French translation of the *Treatise*, in which Leroy for some reason renders Hume's 'string instrument' as *'instrument à percussion'* (ES 150/132). Now, Boundas includes the correct passage in the English translation of *Empiricism and Subjectivity*, but the other occurrences of this remark in Deleuze's texts on Hume do not. We can read, for example, that 'As Hume says, the mind or the imagination does not function, in relation to the passions, like a wind instrument, but like a percussion instrument "where after each stroke the vibrations still retain some sound, which gradually and insensibly decays".'[14]

Matters do not stop there, however, and the phantom percussion instrument can be heard beating throughout Deleuze scholarship.[15] Prefacing their citation of the erroneous text, for example, Amit Rai writes that William James's 'theory of the concatenated union of sensations recalls the empiricism of David Hume, for whom, as Deleuze reminds us, "the mind and its fantasies behave [. . .] in the manner of a percussion instrument"'.[16] Most deliriously of all, Michael Taormina, the translator of the collection *Desert Islands and Other Texts* that includes the 'Hume' encyclopaedia piece where the percussion instrument features also includes a note, attributed to Elie During, that points out that 'Either Deleuze or Hume's French translator mistakenly has "percussion instrument" for the original "string instrument".'[17] This correction qualifies the use of the incorrect translation, but leaves the initial fiction intact.

If this little scene is ironic, it is because it repeats all of the lessons of Deleuze's Hume: that the distinction between truth and falsity is not marked in ideas themselves; that the delirious drifting from the former to the latter and the ramifications of such fictions echo and enlarge themselves through their repetition in language; but that this fiction takes on a positive character by being incorporated into the prosecution of practical life. After all, the mistaken invocation of the percussion instrument *is still a true metaphor*, one that aids us in our reading of both Hume and Deleuze.

TIME AND THE BODY

After a brief discussion of what constitutes 'the absolute essence of empiricism' (ES 92/87), to which we will return in the next chapter, the remaining two-score pages of the eponymously entitled chapter of *Empiricism and Subjectivity* develop a complex analysis of the differences between the mind (as indifferent collection of ideas) and the subject. Here we find Deleuze as a reader of Hume at his most subtle but also his most elliptical, eccentric and telegraphic. Indeed, to elaborate all of the points he makes here would take up an amount of space disproportionate to the significance of the analysis, at least in the context of this book.[18]

Deleuze first of all considers the pre-subjective mind (mind as collection) from three points of view: in relation to temporality, in relation to the body (and more specifically, in relation to the sense-organs), and on its own terms, that is, in terms of the imagination. Having done this, he pursues the same triple perspective from the point of view of the constituted subject. In sum, he presents us with the mind, the body and time as they are before and then after the process of the constitution of the subject. Moreover, in relation to the subject, Deleuze will be more specific yet again, addressing not just, for instance, time and subjectivity, but the way in which this conjunction is played out in belief and morality respectively.[19]

Taken together, then, we arrive at a nine-part analysis of the passage from mind to the subject. Whereas the account of the subject in terms of reflection that we have just seen provides the schema of Deleuze's account, this analysis puts a great deal of flesh on its bones. Let us begin, with Deleuze, by discussing the significance in the unaffected mind of time, the body and the imagination itself.

The mind and the imagination. The terrain Deleuze covers here is already familiar to us. The mind and the imagination are one and the same thing, so long as we note that these terms are used 'not to designate a faculty or a principle of organisation, but rather a particular set or a particular collection' (ES 93/87). This also means, of course, that 'The mind itself is not a subject, nor does it require a subject whose mind it would be' (ES 94/88), and we can recognise in these two latter options the psychological and Kantian accounts of subjectivity.

Now, we know that the collection that forms the mind is a collection of discrete ideas, and in recapitulating this point in the context of the discussion of subjectivity Deleuze notes an important detail. To call perceptions discrete atoms is to speak as if they constituted *spatial* minima. But in fact, we can always imagine objects with a smaller extension than those we perceive – and not only that, we are capable of forming ideas of these objects, reasoning about their relative size, and so on.

This apparent counter-example to Hume's empiricist commitments is displaced the moment that we grasp the fact that the atomic perceptions are the objects of experience themselves. These latter do not possess any intrinsic spatial characteristics whatsoever – indeed, they do not possess extension in any way. Here again is the point at which Hume definitively breaks with Locke and the primary/secondary distinction, since while perceptions have no physical extension, they are always 'visible and tangible, coloured and solid' (ES 98/91). That is, the atoms of experience possess secondary qualities alone. We must conclude, therefore, that spatiality is only found 'in the arrangement of visible or tangible objects', that is, that 'the given is not in space; space is in the given' (ES 99/91).

The mind and the body. At this point, a certain common-sense problem is entertained by both Hume and Deleuze. It is all well and good to insist on the incapacity to reach beyond impressions of sensations and discover their causes in the physical world, but does not the fact that we have such impressions mean that we have some kind of sensory organs?

Deleuze's response is clear: 'the given, the mind, the collection of perceptions cannot call upon anything other than themselves' (ES 96/89). That is, we must insist again that the only access to reality we have is what we find in the impressions of sensation. While we do have experiences of eyes and ears, the faculties of touch and smell, these experiences themselves are reducible to their component impressions.

The mind and time. What, finally, is the place of temporality in the unreflected mind? Unlike space, it is a feature of all experience, and not just that which arises through sight and touch. On the other hand, like space it constitutes an ordering of perceptions. At the level of the collection, this ordering is very simply a matter of *succession*. While the famous critical attack on the idea of the self makes the point clearly, Deleuze here quotes the following passage (a little out of context) from early in the first book of the *Treatise*: 'For we may observe, that there is a continual succession of perceptions in our mind; so that the idea of time is forever present with us' (T 1.1.5.29). Simple succession is thus the temporal correlate of the indifferent ordering of the collection of perceptions.

The subject and time. These three points made, Deleuze then turns to subjectivity, in a passage we have already mentioned:

> What do we mean when we speak of the subject? We mean that the imagination, having been a collection, becomes now a faculty; the distributed collection becomes now a system. The given is reprised in a movement that transcends it. The mind becomes human nature. The subject invents and believes; *it is synthesis, a synthesis of the mind.* (ES 100/92)

On the back of this recapitulation, a much more detailed set of remarks follows, the first of which extends the analysis of temporality. What, first of all, is the place of time in belief and moral invention? The general point is as follows:

To speak of the subject now is to speak of duration, custom, habit, and anticipation. Anticipation is habit, and habit is anticipation [. . .] Habit is the constitutive root of the subject, and the subject, at root, is the synthesis of time – the synthesis of the present and the past in light of the future. (ES 101/92–3)

The synthesis of time is a topic that will occupy Deleuze's thought at length, in *Difference and Repetition* in particular. The point here is rather more straightforward than these later analyses, even if it presages them. In essence, habit is nothing other than a means for dealing with the future. It is only in the habituated capacity to assimilate new experiences that subjectivity has any substance. This capacity, in turn, is obtained through the experiences of the past and the present. These provide the subject with the materials in relation to which beliefs, sympathies and general interests are a response, but they also constitute the opportunities that the process of reflection takes up in order to engender subjectivity as such. Whatever particularities belong to this or that subject, at the most general formal level, the subject is the habitual synthesis of time.

This means that the act of belief is at root an act of *anticipation*: 'the synthesis posits the past as a *rule* for the future' (ES 103/94). In fact, this is what is meant by the notion of transcendence. To transcend the given is not to ascend to another ontological level, a superior rank in being, but to go beyond, and to be able to go beyond, the past in the given. The subject transcends by being able to step into the future, and it can do this because the past is not merely the collection of ideas of past impressions (i.e. memories), but now, according to this synthesis, the means for the installation of habituated tendencies.

The case of morality is similar, and it is once again a matter of anticipation, a certain habitual link to the future: 'each man *expects* to conserve what he already possesses' (ES 101/93). Just as there is no subject unless there is a way of extending its current associations into the future, there can be no object – no *property* – without this being extended forward into time through the creation of institutions.

The subject and the body. How does the body appear from the point of view of subjectivity rather than the mind? Here, Deleuze's remarks are even briefer and somewhat more cryptic. He distinguishes between two further effects that the principles of human nature give rise to.

On the one hand, there is what he calls the '*spontaneity of relation*' (ES 106/96), which is the particular product of the principles of association – or to be more precise, this spontaneity is nothing other than the projection of the subject's transcending activity into the physical world. As Deleuze writes, 'the body is the subject itself envisaged from the point of view of the spontaneity of the relations that, under the influence of the principles, it establishes between ideas'. So, while 'The mechanism of the body cannot explain the spontaneity of the subject' (ES 96/89), the inverse is nevertheless true: the subject in its spontaneity makes use of the category of the body to explain the presupposed origins of unified phenomena – that is, the origin of beliefs qua complex ideas. In this first case, we think the body in the image of a *passive, receptive object*.

On the other hand, there is a '*spontaneity of disposition*' (ES 107/97). Whereas the spontaneity of relations figured by the image of the body give a retrospective consistency to my beliefs – an origin or locus – the spontaneity of disposition gives to my passions an original agent, a bodily cause. 'The impressions of reflection are defined by means of a spontaneity or a disposition and are referred to the body as the biological source of this spontaneity' (ES 107/97). The dispositions in question are nothing other than the passions themselves – thirst and sexual desire, joy and sadness – impressions of reflection that find in the body their source: we assert that 'nature has given to the body certain appetites and inclinations' (T 2.2.6.6). In this case, then, we grasp the body in the image of an *active, desiring subject*, where its activities consist in the set of tendencies that we associate with it, tendencies that are the elements of the moral subject.

THE CONTENT OF SUBJECTIVITY

Now, even once these further elaborations around time and the body are taken into account, the fact is that Deleuze's reading of Hume remains abstract. The form and process proper to subjectivity has been presented to us, but we have not once – beyond certain more or less superficial examples – discussed the particularity of subjects, that is, the particular content of subjectivity in any given case. How can we account for 'the difference between one mind and another?' (ES 115/103).

In fact, we have already seen the direction in which Hume's analysis will have to move. If the principles of association and the passions give the mind order and engender within it the subject, the two do not function with the same degree of abstraction. Association for its part is entirely neutral to circumstance, that is, to particularity. Its field of deployment is ultimately that of the possible and the probable – that is, the hypothetical. If morality like belief begins with a certain state of affairs, and first engenders a certain abstract generality, the subsequent proliferation of general rules all press in the direction of the particular, towards a casuistry and the constraints of the case, as we have seen.

> Everything takes place as if the principles of association provided the subject with its necessary form, whereas the principles of the passions provided it with its singular content. The latter function as the principle for the individuation of the subject. This duality, however, does not signify an opposition between the singular and the universal. The principles of the passions are no less universal or constant than the others. (ES 116–17/104)

Nevertheless, even if the principles of human nature necessarily go beyond the given, there is always a particular given state of affairs. This is what Hume calls *circumstance*, the sequence of contingent events that engender within us particular impressions, and thus the ideas that we consequently possess. Circumstances are 'the variables that define our passions and our interests', and 'a set of circumstances always individuates a subject, since it represents a state of its passions and needs, an allocation of its interests, a distribution of its beliefs and exhilarations' (ES 115/103). In fact, Deleuze's choice of the term 'represents' here is unfortunate. It is rather the case that the subject embodies, in an expanded and always newly invigorated way, the set of circumstances from which it is born.

We could in fact say, conversely, that the principles of human nature 'define laws in which circumstances only act as variables' (ES 117/104). From this point of view, which concentrates our attention on the constitutive role of the principles, it is clear that 'Nature is what history does not explain, what cannot be defined, what may even be useless to describe, or what is common in the most diverse ways of satisfying a tendency' (ES 33–4/44). However, what history does explain, in general and with regard to each particular circumstance, is the primacy of circumstance, the contingent events whose impact on us fires the machinery of the principles. And the ultimate justification for Hume's new science of the mind, for Deleuze, can only be history – 'the true science of human motivation' (ES 34/45) – since it is only history that 'exhibits the uniformity of the human passions' (ES 2/22).

A final point about the subject can now be emphasised. We have seen that subjectivity is constituted through the impressions of reflection, through the haloes of secondary impressions that the principles of human nature give rise to. But we have also seen that impressions of reflection are quintessentially passional, that is, affective in character.

To this we can add the final reason for the primacy of practical reason in Hume, namely the essential place given to circumstance. Not only is the system of the understanding practically inert, and not only is the subject for whom the understanding provides a network of possible institutional models constituted through second-order impressions arising from the passions and not from reason. The material that gives to the principles of human nature their final *raison d'être* is the material of a social, affective life. Since 'the subject cannot be separated from the singular content which is strictly essential to it, it is because subjectivity is essentially *practical*' (ES 117/104). Deleuze will not hesitate to call this 'the fundamental claim of empiricism' (ES 117/104), and it is to this link between empiricism and a practical subjectivity that we will finally turn to now.

NOTES

1. Norman Kemp Smith, *The Philosophy of David Hume* (Basingstoke: Palgrave, [1941] 2005), v.
2. Gilles Deleuze, *What is Grounding?*, trans. Arjen Kleinherenbrink, ed. Tony Yanick, Jason Adams and Mohammad Salemy (Grand Rapids: &&& Publishing, 2015), 4.
3. This is particularly true given the self-critique advanced by Hume in the Appendix he added to the *Treatise* when it was first published in full (i.e. with the third book 'On Morals' included). He famously writes there that 'there are two principles, which I cannot render consistent; nor is it in my powers to renounce either of them, viz. *that all our distinct perceptions are distinct existences*, and *that the mind never perceives any real connexion among distinct existences*' (T App 19). This assertion has always puzzled Hume's readers, and justifiably so, since not only are the two assertions perfectly compatible on their own terms, the bulk of Book I of the *Treatise* relies upon the conclusions that they lead to together. Deleuze seems to conceive of subjectivity as he elaborates it to be the solution of this problem (at ES 32), that is, that the problem is not so serious for Hume as Hume seems to think that it is. This has led at least one critic to conclude that Deleuze's systematisation of Hume goes much too far and pays too little attention to its own inconsistencies. In a remark that footnotes the passage from the Appendix just cited, Patricia De Martelaere says of Deleuze's reading that 'he outlines a global framework in which all of the elements of this [Hume's] philosophy – even the most problematic, those that Hume's own system, as he himself had to recognize, were powerless to resolve' (Patricia De Martelaere, 'Gilles Deleuze, interprète de Hume', *Revue Philosophique de Louvain* 82:54 (1984), 224). We will return to De

Martelaere's critique of Deleuze's Hume below when it comes to the role of impressions of reflection in subjectivity (see note 10). But on this particular point, the criticism seems unfair. Not only is the precise meaning of Hume's self-critique difficult to establish – Don Garrett goes so far as to say that 'no commentator has ever simply endorsed the answer of any other commentator' (Don Garrett, 'Rethinking Hume's Second Thoughts about Personal Identity', in *The Possibility of Philosophical Understanding*, ed. Jason Bridges, Niko Kolodny and Wai-Hung Wong (Oxford: Oxford University Press, 2011), 16) – it is not even precisely clear that subjectivity is what is at stake. For a reading that emphasises instead the phrase 'the intellectual world', and which argues that subjectivity is in fact not at stake at all in the Appendix passage, see Corliss Gayda Swain, 'Personal Identity and the Sceptical System of Philosophy', in *The Blackwell Guide to Hume's* Treatise, ed. Saul Traiger (Oxford: Blackwell, 2006), 133–50.

4. In this text, and at a couple of other moments (e.g. ES 119), Constantin Boundas translates Deleuze's *se constituer* as 'to constitute itself'. This is, I think, a somewhat misleading rendering: the fact that the subject is a product means that it cannot constitute itself. The problem is most striking in the following passage: 'As a result, we see that the principles of the passions must be combined with the principles of association in order for the subject to constitute itself within the mind [*On voit donc que les principes de la passion doivent s'unir aux principes d'association pour que le sujet se constitue dans l'esprit*]' (ES 116/103). Moreover, since, as we know, the principles are only registered in the mind through their effects, it would be impossible for them to be combined *by* the subject in an act of self-constitution. The same misprision leads to a confusion in the penultimate sentence of the book, which reads '*La philosophie doit se constituer comme la théorie de ce que nous faisons, non pas comme la théorie de ce qui est*' (ES 152/133), which we will render 'We must constitute philosophy as a theory of what we do, and not a theory of what there is.' All of this said, it is important to recognise that, because subjectivity is defined as a gradual process of transcendence – transcendence of the collection of perceptions in the mind – we are not dealing with a simple two-step process but rather an intertwined two-level structure,

such that it is true both that 'the subject transcends itself', and that 'Subject is that which develops itself' (ES 85). All of these points will be returned to above.

5. Immanuel Kant, *Critique of Pure Reason*, trans. and ed. Paul Guyer and Allen W. Wood (Cambridge: Cambridge University Press, 1997), A22/B37.

6. Kant, *Critique of Pure Reason*, A111.

7. Kant, *Critique of Pure Reason*, A100–10.

8. Kant, *Critique of Pure Reason*, A100–1.

9. Gilles Deleuze, *Kant's Critical Philosophy*, trans. Hugh Tomlinson and Barbara Habberjam (London: Athlone, 1984), 12–13.

10. It is at this very point that Patricia De Martelaere's critical reading of *Empiricism and Subjectivity* appears weakest. She writes that 'What [. . .] appears to me indefensible is Deleuze's assimilation of impressions of reflection to *the effects of the principles*' (De Martelaere, 'Gilles Deleuze, interprète de Hume', 241). Now, it is true that at least on one occasion Deleuze appears to make precisely this kind of claim, in the following text cited by De Martelaere: 'the effect of the principles is always an impression of reflection' (ES 113). But to say that the principles *always* have this effect is not to say that they *only* have such an effect. As we have just seen, the principles of human nature have two orders of effect that are not mutually exclusive. As Deleuze puts it shortly after the passage cited above, 'We can in fact see that there are two ways of defining the principle: within the collection, the principle elects, chooses, designates, and invites certain impressions of sensation among others; having done this, it constitutes impressions of reflection in connection with these elected impressions. Thus, it has two roles at the same time: a selective role and a constitutive role' (ES 113).

11. Kant, *Critique of Pure Reason*, A100.

12. Deleuze here indicates that he is citing from the *Treatise*, but nothing there appears to precisely correspond to '*advises* certain ideas rather than others'. That said, the sentiment is clearly borne out by numerous passages (see, for one prominent example, T 1.3.1.1).

13. Gilles Deleuze, 'Hume', in *Desert Islands and Other Texts*, ed. David Lapoujade, trans. Michael Taormina (New York: Semiotext(e), 2004), 162–9.

14. Deleuze, 'Hume', 167.
15. Including, it must be said, by the author of this book. See Jon Roffe, 'David Hume', in *Deleuze's Philosophical Lineage* (Edinburgh: Edinburgh University Press, 2009), 70.
16. Amit S. Rai, 'Race and Ontologies of Sensation', in *Deleuze and Race*, ed. Arun Saldanha and Jason Michael Adams (Edinburgh: Edinburgh University Press, 2012), 282. There are many other examples, of course, but the strict identification of this claim with Hume that Rai presents makes it particularly striking.
17. Deleuze, 'Hume', 305n2.
18. Puzzlingly, when Deleuze first lists the three facets of the subject he aims to discuss (time, body, mind), he does so in the opposite order in which he discusses them. Here, we have followed the order of the actual discussion.
19. In fact, things are more complicated yet again, since Deleuze also indicates that he wants to consider these three facets of subjectivity from four points of view. That is, in relation to the subject (1) in terms of the imagination, (2) in terms of temporality and (3) in terms of the body, Deleuze proposes to consider four questions: 'What are the characteristics of the subject in the case of belief [. . .] and invention?'; 'By means of which principles is the subject constituted in this way?'; and 'What are the various stages of the system [i.e. what are the stages of this constitution]?' (ES 92). In fact, though, Deleuze only addresses the latter two questions implicitly in *Empiricism and Subjectivity*, and the elaboration of what they might involve would take us well beyond the scope of this reconstruction.

6

The Singularity of Empiricism

The opening pages of *Empiricism and Subjectivity* repeat the following sentiment: 'Hume is above all a moralist, a political thinker, and a historian' (ES 17/33). Given the relative status of morality and belief, we already know why this is the case. However, the further one reads into the book, the more it becomes apparent that this a preparatory stance, meant to undermine the epistemological misprision inaugurated by Kant, but one that does not include everything that belongs to Hume's philosophy.

In Deleuze's view, Hume is above all an *empiricist*. On its own terms, such a nomination is uncontroversial, but everything turns around what we take the moniker to mean. The final element of *Empiricism and Subjectivity* that we will examine is thus the intriguing set of remarks that Deleuze makes there about the nature of empiricism as a philosophical position.

But first, a quick word on naturalism. The dominance of the narrow sceptical reading of Hume's philosophy has been the object of serious critical attention for almost a century now, begun by Norman Kemp Smith in his classic 1905 piece, 'The Naturalism of Hume',[1] and pursued in his later *The Philosophy of David Hume*.[2] Smith is the standard bearer for a reading of Hume that displaces the centrality of epistemological questions of the kind that lead us to conclude that Hume's ultimate goal is critical and sceptical. In place of this is an emphasis on practical life as the essential ground upon which epistemological questions can be posed and answered – as Smith memorably puts it, 'it was the through the gateway of morals that Hume entered into his philosophy'.[3]

If this way of reading Hume is worth invoking here, it is to distinguish it, despite all appearances, from Deleuze's approach. It is true that Hume is a naturalist for Deleuze in the sense just indicated. Nevertheless, we can say that the naturalist Hume appears to nevertheless retain too much of Kant's Hume from Deleuze's point of view. To find in Hume a naturalised epistemology (whether merely protean or fully fledged) is to present his philosophy such that it manages to move beyond the sceptical cul-de-sac, but it fails to properly appreciate the constitution of subjectivity that underpins both morality and belief.[4] In this sense, we can say that Deleuze's reading of Hume (whether or not it is judged to be successful) aims to resolve what Paul Russell calls 'the riddle of the *Treatise*'. The riddle concerns the apparent tension between the sceptical strains in Hume's thought on the one hand, and his naturalism on the other. The interpretive solution, as Russell notes, involves demonstrating that 'these (apparently) conflicting themes are an essential aspect or component of some deeper purpose or objective'.[5] For Deleuze, this is the problematic of subjectivity itself, but only once it is approached from the empiricist point of view.

PHILOSOPHY AND THE QUESTION

The chapter devoted to 'The Principles of Human Nature' begins with a sharp, forceful critique of a certain mode of critique. Deleuze identifies a retrograde mode of engagement with the work of philosophers, one that treats their work as essentially reducible to their psycho-social situation. 'What a philosopher *says* is offered as if it were what he *does* or as what he *wants*' (ES 118/105). It is not only Hume that is the victim of this kind of inane critique, Deleuze insist, for 'The case is similar for all great philosophers' (ES 118/105).

If this is the false mode of philosophical critique, its true counterpart consists in a singular focus on the *orienting problem* of the philosophy in question. The only legitimate way to critique a philosopher is immanently, on the terrain that they themselves present us with: 'only one kind of objection is worthwhile: the objection which shows that the question raised by a philosopher is not a good question, that it does not force the nature of things enough, that it should be raised in another way, that we should raise it in a better way, or that we should raise a different question' (ES 120/107).

Consequently, 'we cannot raise against Hume any objections we wish' (ES 120/107). If we want to critique the Humean account, we would need to install ourselves in the question that he poses and test its limits from within. More generally,

> we can see that most of the objections raised against the great philosophers are empty. People say to them: things are not like that. But, in fact, it is not a matter of knowing whether things are like that or not. It is a matter of knowing *whether the question which presents things in such a light is good or not, rigorous or not.* (ES 120/106)

This amounts, to borrow a famous trope from *Difference and Repetition* that this passage presages, to shifting the question of truth and falsity from the answer to the question itself: in philosophy, 'there are no critiques of solutions, there are only critiques of problems' (ES 119/106).[6] Summarily speaking, we might attribute two positive features to a philosophical question as a result, which at the same time provide us with the grounds for its assessment and critique (in philosophy, 'the question and the critique of the question are one' (ES 119/106)): its force, and the internal consistency of its elaboration. The latter corresponds to the internal organisation of the elaboration of the question, while the former describes the capacity of the question to constrain what is to reveal itself in a certain way: 'To put something in question means subordinating and subjecting things to the question, intending, through this constrained and forced subsumption, that they reveal an essence or a nature' (ES 119/106). And indeed, in the final analysis, the systematic coherence of an elaborated question is subordinated to its capacity to force the exposure of an essence or a nature.

Philosophy has an equally singular goal as a result: 'a philosophical theory is an elaborately developed question, and nothing else; by itself and in itself, it is not the resolution to a problem, but the elaboration, *to the very end*, of the necessary implications of a formulated question' (ES /106). While Deleuze will return to the question 'what is philosophy?' throughout his work, this constitutes his first answer, and it retains its salutary force, remains a salutary reminder.[7]

Deleuze adds that, consequently, it is not that we should simply exclude an examination of social and psychological factors in the formulation of a philosophy. These should indeed be taken into account, but only to the extent that they are included in the formulation of the problem that orients it: 'these factors concern nothing other than the question itself, and only in order to provide it with a motivation, without telling us whether it is true or false' (ES 120/106).

If we return to the matter in hand, however, we can say that we can only define empiricism 'through the position of a precise problem, and through the presentation of the conditions of this problem. No other definition is possible' (ES 120/107). As he dispenses with three poor answers to this question, Deleuze draws close to his presentation of empiricism's constitutive dualism, the heart of his definition.

The first option would be to define empiricism as 'the theory according to which knowledge begins only with experience'. For Deleuze, this is the least adequate account, simply 'a piece of nonsense', since – at least in these terms – it is a claim that every major philosopher could assent to, 'Plato and Leibniz included' (ES 121/107). But it is also false for two more substantial reasons. The first is the fact that empiricism is not fundamentally

132

an epistemological doctrine, but a theory of practice: morality is more fundamental than 'knowledge'. The second is that, if we examine what the term 'experience' means (for Hume at least), we see that it means two different things, and neither of them is constitutive of knowledge. On the one hand, experience is simply the collection of perceptions that constitute the mind qua imagination; on the other, experience is the fact that I have had experiences in the past (inscribed in the mind in the form of memories), but here we grasp experience as a principle of human nature – since the fact of having been affected is a ubiquitous feature of the mind. In neither case is there knowledge, or even belief in Hume's sense. We are missing the activity of the principles that allow us to transcend these neutral atoms and transform the mind into an activated structure, and the relations that the principles engender – that is, the structural constituents of belief – 'are not derived from experience' (ES 121/108).

The second option would be to define empiricism in terms of the given, and the correlative passivity of the mind. Clearly, we are much closer to Hume's own views here, but as with 'experience', 'the given' has a double sense in Humean empiricism. The given is first of all the collection of perceptions in the mind. But there is something else: 'in this collection the subject which transcends experience and the relations which do not depend on ideas are also given' (ES 122/108). We will return to the question of relations below, but for now it suffices to say that, in addition to the collection of ideas, we find the two orders of effect of the principles: complex ideas (constituted by relations that arise thanks to the principles of association), and the subject qua immanent habitual organisation of the collection.

Deleuze clearly shifts the terms of his discussion here, since the question 'how is the subject constituted inside the given?' makes no sense if we take the subject to be a part of the given in the sense that Deleuze uses the term elsewhere in *Empiricism and Subjectivity*. But the key point he is making here still holds – to merely invoke the passive receptivity of the mind and the affections constituted by impressions and ideas cannot by itself encompass Humean empiricism. The given is doubled by the subject. This amounts to saying that Hume's philosophy is irreducible to a psychological mereology, and it is a conclusion that is presupposed by the lynchpin role of morality in Hume's system, in which the subject is itself the lynchpin.

THE EMPIRICIST DUALISM

We should note in passing that that the options we have just canvassed encompass the sceptical Hume and the naturalist Hume, and show the need to pass beyond what they offer us – to the *empiricist* Hume that interests Deleuze. What exactly is this? While the remarks above imply the answer, it remains something of a surprise: 'empiricism will not be correctly defined except by means of a dualism' (ES 122/108).

Like transcendence, 'dualism' is a term that, with its Cartesian overtones, would seem to be anathema to Deleuze's philosophy. As with transcendence, though, everything turns around the register in which 'dualism' is used.

What distinguishes Hume from Kant, let us recall, is his insistence on the fact that the contents of the mind are not natively subject to the principles that will come to organise them – impressions and their corresponding ideas are not phenomena. Consequently, the Humean dualism is not between phenomena and noumena, since it lies entirely within the mind. Or, better, Hume locates this famous Kantian distinction within the mind itself.

In its most straightforward acceptation, then, the empiricist dualism concerns the split between the mind and the subject. While Deleuze provides a series of interrelated definitions – 'between terms and relations, or more exactly between the causes of perceptions and the causes of relations, between the hidden powers of nature and the principles of human nature' (ES 123/109) – this is the essential point.

Now, during his discussion of the nature of philosophy, Deleuze writes that 'empiricism is definable [. . .] only through the position of a precise problem, and through the presentation of the conditions of this problem' (ES 121/107). We know the question, Hume's question, well: how is the subject constituted inside the given? But we can now add that the condition under which this question is posed is nothing other than the empiricist dualism between nature and human nature – from this 'the problem of the subject, as it is formulated in empiricism, follows' (ES 109/98). We see the sense of calling this the condition of the empiricist problem: it is only against the backdrop of this dualism that the problem gains sense. If we identify the subject with the collection of ideas, then there is no problem – even if this is a particularly feeble position. And if we subordinate both the collection and the subject to the same principles, as Kant does, the problem does not appear either. It is only because there is this division that Hume's philosophy gains consistency, focus and force.

Thanks to this framework we can give, following Deleuze, an example of what a good critique would look like, since this is just what Kant does in relation to the Humean set-up. Kant agrees, first of all, that the imagination is the correct terrain to raise the problem of the formation of belief, and thus installs himself in Hume's question. But, from this point of view, he problematises this question at what is its weakest point, the point that limits its scope and force. If there were only a contingent accord between nature and human nature – if, that is, the empiricist dualism underpins the posing of the question – then there would never be a chance that belief could ever eventuate: 'our empirical imagination would never get to do anything suitable to its capacity, and would thus remain hidden in the interior of the mind, like a dead and to us unknown faculty'.[8]

'RELATIONS ARE EXTERNAL TO THEIR TERMS'

It is time to address the very famous characterisation of empiricism that Deleuze first presents in *Empiricism and Subjectivity* and repeats a number of times later in his work. This is the claim that, for empiricism, 'relations are external to their terms' (ES 63/66, 109/99, 113/101, 139/123).[9]

And indeed, while I have just claimed that the empiricist dualism is what conditions the question of subjectivity, Deleuze himself says more specifically that Hume 'presents the conditions of possibility of the question and those of its critique in the following terms: *relations are external to ideas*' (ES 120/107).

Relations are the products of the principles of association, that is, the qualifications of ideas in the mind that the principles give rise to. Hume identifies two kinds of relation. According to a famous text in the first *Enquiry*, 'All reasonings may be divided into two kinds, namely, demonstrative reasoning, or that concerning relations of ideas, and moral reasoning, or that concerning matter of fact and existence' (EHU 1.30). In Deleuze's view, this distinction – which came to be known as Hume's fork – is the latter-day rendition of the distinction presented in the *Treatise* between natural and philosophical relations.

It is important to note right from the outset that Deleuze considers the distinction between the two forms of relation to be subordinate to the thesis of relational exteriority. In proceeding in this way, he definitively rejects a claim first advanced by Kant in the *Prolegomena*, but still widely held in Hume scholarship today, according to which demonstrative reasoning turns around analytic truths.

But let us begin with natural relations, which constitute complex ideas about experience, or factual beliefs: 'sending that ill-advised poem set off the chain of events that would lead to her leaving me', 'she was sitting, crookedly, on the red chair', 'before the break-up, she watched the storm'. Beliefs about matters of fact are collections of ideas qualified by temporal, spatial and causal relations, and by the relation of identity. Clearly, none of these relations can be derived from the woman in question, and nothing about the idea of her necessarily includes her sitting in this or that way, initiating a break-up or watching a storm before doing so.

On the other hand, demonstrative reasoning compares particular ideas with one another according to relations of 'resemblance, degrees of quality, and propositions of quantity and number' (ES 109/99). When I write, for instance, '7 + 5 = 12', relations of relative quantity and equality are invoked. It is here that the common interpretation, first stated by Kant, takes root. For it does seem that, in arithmetic, if not also geometry (whose imprecision Hume dwells on at length in the *Treatise*; see T 1.1.4), the relations that hold between the discrete ideas are secondary to the ideas themselves. Presumably, so the reasoning goes, this is also why Hume states of demonstrative reasoning that it 'depend[s] entirely on the ideas we compare together' (T 1.3.1.1).

If this interpretation is true, then Deleuze's exclamation 'relations are external to their terms' has a very limited scope indeed. But this is not at all the case. To illustrate this point, Deleuze invokes the case of equality, which figures in basic arithmetic and seems to turn around the characteristics of the ideas in question. For example, in the equation 7 + 5 = 12, it appears that the relations derive their validity from the terms: it is only because 7 and 5 together add up to 12 that the sign of equality = holds true. But as far as Hume is concerned, this is false: 'let us consider, that since equality is a relation, it is not, strictly speaking, a property in the figures themselves, but arises merely from the comparison, which the mind makes betwixt them' (T 1.2.4.21). In other words, experience and the deployment of the principles of association are required in order for the production of this relation of equality. While it is true that this relation 'depend[s] entirely on the ideas which we compare together' (T 1.3.1.1), this is not to say that the truth of equality inheres in the quantities 7, 5 and 12, but that when the relation varies, so too must the terms. It means that there is more than one possible 'system of *operations*' (ES 111/100), into which the terms might enter. The fact that the equality relation is one of these does not in any way follow analytically from the terms themselves.

But we could also cite an emblematic passage from the *Treatise* concerning the notion of the shortest line (what Hume calls here a right line):

> mathematicians pretend they give an exact definition of a right line, when they say, it is the shortest way betwixt two points. But in the first place I observe, that this is more properly the discovery of one of the properties of a right line, than a just deflation of it. For I ask any one, if upon mention of a right line he thinks not immediately on such a particular appearance, and if it is not by accident only that he considers this property? A right line can be comprehended alone; but this definition is unintelligible without a comparison with other lines, which we conceive to be more extended. In common life it is established as a maxim, that the straightest way is always the shortest; which would be as absurd as to say, the shortest way is always the shortest, if our idea of a right line was not different from that of the shortest way betwixt two points. (T 1.2.4.27)[10]

The definition of the straight line as the shortest path between two points is thus not a simple idea, an analytic truth, but the product of experience and the operation of the principles. By itself, the shortest line is just a line, and in order to provide it with the qualification that it is 'the shortest', we require an effort of comparison, that is, synthesis, and one that is only possible thanks to the materials furnished by experience, and the activity of the principles of association that give rise to the relations that allow us to compare them.

In light of these points, Kant's criticisms of Hume appear in all their idiosyncrasy. At the key moment in the *Prolegomena* on this front, he writes that, according to Hume,

> Pure mathematics contains only *analytic* propositions, but metaphysics contains synthetic propositions *a priori*. Now he erred severely in this, and this error had decisively damaging consequences for his entire conception. For had he not done this, he would have expanded his question about the origin of our synthetic judgments far beyond his metaphysical concept

of causality and extended it also to the possibility of *a priori* mathematics; for he would have had to accept mathematics as synthetic as well. But then he would by no means have been able to found his metaphysical propositions on mere experience, for otherwise he would have had to subject the axioms of pure mathematics to experience as well, which he was much too reasonable to do.[11]

The irony here – if we follow Deleuze's reading – is that Hume indeed proceeds just as Kant suggests he ought to have. But he also goes so far as to invoke experience as the foundation of mathematics and its axioms, as the discussion of the line we have just seen clearly demonstrates

But now we need to ask to what degree Deleuze's claim that 'relations are external to their terms' can be the watchword for empiricism *tout court*. And in fact, this thesis can only be a subordinate one, since it belongs wholly to the order of belief: 'Relations are the *effect* of the principles of association' (ES 111/100). It cannot, consequently, constitute a condition for moral invention. Deleuze himself makes this point:

> The principles of association establish natural relations among ideas forming inside the mind an entire network similar to a system of channels. [. . .] Hume, however, makes an important remark: were the mind fixed in this way only, there will never be, nor could there ever have been, morality [. . .] Being external to their terms, how would relations be able to determine the priority of one term over the other, or the subordination of one to the other? But it is obvious that action does not tolerate such an equivocation [. . .] Relations, by themselves, would suffice to make the action eternally possible, but they cannot account for the actual performance of the action. (ES 139/123)

Put another way, Deleuze's claim that the thesis of the externality of relations is the paradigmatic form of the empiricism dualism is too specific.[12] We must always recall that, for Hume, morality pays for all, and in morality, 'It is no longer a matter of fixed relations, but of centers of fixation' (ES 140/124).

139

Where does this leave Deleuze's famous remark then? It is perhaps best to see it as a kind of critical discriminant, a filter according to which we can distinguish between empiricist and non-empiricist positions, as Deleuze indicates at one point (ES 123/109). It is a necessary component of empiricist philosophy but can in no way be counted as sufficient. Ultimately, it would be better – more inclusive, bear a greater philosophical force – to make the empiricist dualism, which includes the opposition between relations and terms as a particular case, the condition for the problem of posing the empiricist question. Only in this way would Hume's philosophy seem able to be included under the heading of 'empiricism' as Deleuze defines it.

PHILOSOPHY AS THE THEORY OF PRACTICE

The question of subjectivity and its conditions together appear, in many respects, to provide a summary of empiricism that fits the reading of Hume proposed in *Empiricism and Subjectivity*, bar the final link: what is the nature of the relationship between empiricism and subjectivity itself? It is here that we find the gravitational centre of Deleuze's reading of Hume.

We can begin by briefly recapitulating the movement of the analysis so far. Belief is first of all subordinate to morality, and to the social life that constitutes the latter's extension: 'association is *for the sake of the passions*' (ES 150/132). Correlatively, the critical and comparative activity of theoretical reason, neutral on its own terms, finds its *raison d'être* in social existence, as the means for the production of institutional models. But, second, we know that beliefs and interests are not produced in the mind as so many disconnected particularities, but are the expressive features of an activated subjectivity. This subjectivity is essentially passional, since it finds its origins in impressions of reflection, second-order refractions of the affections of pleasure and pain. As we have seen, it is this second point that ultimately explains the first. The passional subject, born from the affects of the mind, requires the principles of association, but only in order to provide an ordered set of connections that the practical, moral life charges with interests and puts to use. Finally, there is the role of circumstance, the specific affective content that gives rise to this particular subject.

For Deleuze, the thread that runs through the whole analysis is that subjectivity is not a fixed structure, but an aleatory adventure. This is why he will write that

> The fact that there is no theoretical subjectivity, and that there cannot be one, becomes the fundamental claim of empiricism. And, if we examine it closely, it is merely another way of saying that the subject is constituted within the given. If the subject is constituted within the given, then, in fact, there is only a practical subject. (ES 117/104)

At first blush, and despite its opposition with the theoretical, the modifier 'practical' here appears to simply mean 'contingent'. But Deleuze's point is that the contingent and the practical come to the same thing in the subject. What is contingent in subjectivity is that affective bedrock of the mind that only becomes subject as it becomes social, moral (in the expanded sense) and political. This is why, right at the end of *Empiricism and Subjectivity*, Deleuze states that 'We must constitute philosophy as the theory of what we are doing, not as a theory of what there is' (ES 152/133).

The theory of the subject and the formulation of empiricism arrive at the same point, and really, are the same point from two complementary points of view since they both proceed from the empiricist dualism itself.

THE PLACE OF PURPOSIVENESS

In light of all this, we must touch again on the category of purposiveness. If empiricism is a theory of practice, this notion would seem to be particularly out of place, and even to characterise it merely as the emptiest moment in Hume's empiricism as Deleuze does seems insufficient.

It is true that the belief in a pre-established harmony between nature and human nature must be presupposed from within Hume's system. Without it, to paraphrase Kant, neither experience nor subjectivity could ever begin to unfold. We must hold an implicit belief in

> a kind of pre-established harmony between the course of nature and the succession of our ideas; and though the powers and forces by which the former is governed, be wholly unknown to us; yet our thoughts and conceptions have still, we find, gone on in the same train with the other works of nature. (EHU 2.44)

It is also for this reason that Deleuze will go so far as to write that 'The problem of this accord provides empiricism with a real metaphysics, that is, with the problem of purposiveness: what kind of accord is there between the collection of ideas and the association of ideas' (ES 123/109).

Very well. But as Deleuze himself puts it a few years later: 'Hume's response was coherent, but it does not teach us anything and remains disquieting on the part of an author who attacks the idea of God.'[13] How can this concern be resolved? The passage from the end of *Empiricism and Subjectivity* I cited in part a moment ago in fact reads in full as follows:

> as we believe and invent, we make of the given itself a *Nature*. At this point Hume's philosophy reaches its ultimate point: Nature conforms to being. Human nature conforms to nature – but in what sense? Within the given, we establish relations and we form totalities. But these do not depend on the given, but rather on the principles we know, which are purely functional. And these functions agree with the hidden powers on which the given depends, but which we do not know. We call 'purposiveness' this accord between intentional finality and nature. This accord can only be thought; and it is doubtless the emptiest and most impoverished of thoughts. We must constitute philosophy as the theory of what we are doing, not as a theory of what there is. What we do has its principles; and Being can never be grasped but as the object of a synthetic relation with the very principles of what we do. (ES 152/133)

This passage, the last in *Empiricism and Subjectivity*, is remarkable for the way it switches perspectives, not once but three times. Purposiveness is first the ultimate point of Hume's philosophy, and then 'the emptiest and most impoverished of thoughts', before seemingly being dismissed altogether with the sentiment that philosophy *should* not contemplate being itself. But the final sentence contains the most puzzling accent of all.

It would seem that here, in the final moment of *Empiricism and Subjectivity*, that a third meaning of empiricist philosophy appears. The first told us that empiricism is defined by the question 'how is the subject constituted within the given?', and the second that empiricism must be oriented solely by practice – that is, it must only be the theory of intersubjective practice of passional integration. For the first, purposiveness is a necessary by-product of the dualism that conditions it, while for the second it appears as a rebuke, something in need of repression. But the last claim presents us with a third, meta-theoretical perspective.

At stake here is no longer practice itself, a practical subjectivity, but the theory of that practice, and from this point of view, the problematic of purposiveness is best conceived as a theoretical supplement. The theory of practice and the theory of being are mutually intertwined. We cannot directly analyse the latter, because it only manifests itself as an inner foreign element that emerges along with the former, an irregularity in the selvedge of the empiricist theory of the practical subject. So it is not, strictly speaking, that we should provide no theory of what there is, but that this theory must always be yoked together with an attention to the principles, qua principles of practice.

From this point of view, Deleuze's remark in the 'What is Grounding?' lectures that implies a lingering theism – or its immediate consequence, or its near analogue – in Hume's thought would be rejected by the Deleuze of *Empiricism and Subjectivity*. What purposiveness names, for empiricism, is the small, peculiar aperture that it possesses on being qua being.

Ontology attains validity only as the shadow of philosophical anthropology, and contrary to Bergson's famous edict, the empiricist must always attempt to show the dark beneath the light.[14] The problematic of purposiveness must only be seen, and can only properly be seen, out of the corner of the eye. The moment that it becomes an object of investigation on its own terms, the Humean philosopher joins Parmenides and Democritus, Berkeley and Locke in promulgating fictions, conjuring 'spectres in the dark' (T 1.4.4.1). In this last act, empiricism appears as akin to an optical discipline, a matter of focus and framing – the empiricist as director of photography.

The reflection on the very last words of *Empiricism and Subjectivity* returns us to its very first words – its peculiar dedication to the great French Hegelian 'Jean Hyppolite, a sincere and respectful homage'. In a review of Hyppolite's *Logic and Existence* published a year after Deleuze's Hume book, we find Deleuze endorsing the vision of philosophy presented by his master, according to which '*Philosophy must be ontology, it cannot be anything else; but there is no ontology of essence, there is only an ontology of sense.*'[15] Aside from the rejection of the category of essence, there is little here that resembles the Hume of *Empiricism and Subjectivity*. Indeed, a few lines further on, Deleuze even adds that 'If Hyppolite's thesis "philosophy is ontology" means one thing above all, it is that philosophy is not anthropology.'[16]

The two near-contemporaneous texts appear at odds with one another, but in fact Deleuze's reading of Hyppolite already includes the means by which he will eventually break with the entire structure of purposiveness, or, to be more precise, it includes the means to maintain the entirety of the empiricist position that Deleuze develops in *Empiricism and Subjectivity* while ejecting purposiveness. In the review, Deleuze poses a now-familiar problematic:

we have to understand what being is with respect to the given. Being, according to Hyppolite, is not *essence* but *sense*. Saying that this world is sufficient not only means that it [is] sufficient *for us*, but that it is sufficient *unto itself* and that the world refers to being not as the essence beyond appearances, and not as a second world which would be the world of the Intelligible, but as the sense of this world.[17]

In light of this, we might say that the importance of Hyppo-lite for Deleuze's reading of Hume is that he shows the way in which the empiricist dualism is deficient on its own terms. But this is too shallow a reading – Hume is nothing if not hostile to any form of substance metaphysics. The interpretation of the final passage in *Empiricism and Subjectivity* that we entertained above is only possible if we identify Being and 'what there is' according to a certain substance metaphysics that seems to be latent in the notion of purposiveness. But if we identify Being with a differential field of sense, then this conclusion no longer follows. Instead, a synthetic relationship between sense and practice would become the true object of philosophical reflection. This line of thinking, prevalent in a variety of ways throughout Deleuze's work, is perhaps best expressed in his final published essay, 'Immanence: A Life . . .', where the subject and the object are *both* transcendent in relation to a prior immanent field.

But these remarks already go beyond the purpose of the current study. They are meant only to show that there is a path that *Empiricism and Subjectivity* leaves open, and the one that is effectively framed by Hyppolite's reading of Hegel, which is the one that Deleuze takes up in his later work, even though it effectively turns Hume's position inside out like a worn glove.

NOTES

1. Norman Kemp Smith, 'The Naturalism of Hume', *Mind* 14:54 (1905), 149–73. It is worth noting that, title aside, the term 'naturalism' does not appear in the 1905 article, somewhat justifying the critical assessment given in Joseph Agassi, 'A Note on Smith's Term "Naturalism"', *Hume Studies* 12:1 (1986), 92–8.

2. Norman Kemp Smith, *The Philosophy of David Hume* (Basingstoke: Palgrave, [1941] 2005).
3. Smith, *The Philosophy of David Hume*, vi.
4. In his critical examination of *Empiricism and Subjectivity*, Fosl rightly notes that a more recent trend in Hume scholarship is closer to Deleuze's reading: 'these scholars have begun to liberate themselves from the notion that Book I of the *Treatise* and the *Enquiry Concerning the Principles of Understanding* constitutes the essence – the defining frame of reference, one might say – of Hume's thought, a standard against which Hume's other writings must be understood either as elaborations (as in the case of his moral texts) or as digressions (e.g. his historical project and essays). This later generation has begun to examine Hume's work more holistically and in doing so has shifted the center of hermeneutic gravity so that Hume appears now less of a naturalizing epistemologist/psychologist and more of a philosophical historian, sociologist, and moralist' (Peter S. Fosl, 'Empiricism, Difference, and Common Life', *Man and World* 26:3 (1993), 320). Here, the difference with Deleuze is a more subtle one, and turns around an insistence on the *philosophical* character of Hume's work, and consequently the way in which he engages with history, society and morality will be philosophical in character. The first chapter of *Empiricism and Subjectivity* plays this down, but as its argument gains in complexity, Deleuze more and more insists on its irreducibility. Thus Hume is not straightforwardly a historian, sociologist or moralist, but a philosopher engaged with the problem on which all of these fields of enquiry converge, the problem of subjectivity itself.
5. Paul Russell, *The Riddle of Hume's Treatise: Scepticism, Naturalism and Irreligion* (Oxford: Oxford University Press, 2010), 7.
6. See Gilles Deleuze, *Difference and Repetition*, trans. Paul Patton (New York: Columbia University Press, 1995), 157–61: 'Sense is located in the problem itself . . .' (157).
7. There is a tantalising moment in these same passages where the distinction between science and philosophy that is elaborated in *What is Philosophy?* seems to first appear. Deleuze considers whether philosophy could be defined as 'a response to a set of problems' (ES 119/106). His answer is striking: 'Undoubtedly, this explanation

has the advantage, at least, of locating the necessity for a theory in relation to something that can serve as its foundation. But this relation would be scientific rather than philosophical [. . .] a philosophical theory is an elaborately developed question, and nothing else' (ES 119/106). Here, I would argue, we find the first version of the concept-immanence, function-reference *dispositif* elaborated in the final work. Everywhere, this 'answers to the big questions' vision of philosophy leads only to the vacuous circulation of opinions. If all philosophy is not to fall foul of this mode of thought, the terrain of engagement must be shifted; we must turn to 'the pedagogy of the concept' (Gilles Deleuze and Félix Guattari, *What is Philosophy?*, trans. Hugh Tomlinson and Graham Burchell (New York: Columbia University Press, 1996), 12).

8. Immanuel Kant, *Critique of Pure Reason*, trans. and ed. Paul Guyer and Allen W. Wood (Cambridge: Cambridge University Press, 1997), A100.

9. See for example Gilles Deleuze, 'Hume', in *Desert Islands and Other Texts*, ed. David Lapoujade, trans. Michael Taormina (New York: Semiotext(e), 2004), 163; and Gilles Deleuze and Claire Parnet, *Dialogues*, trans. Hugh Tomlinson and Barbara Habberjam (New York: Columbia University Press, 1987), 55–7. See also Deleuze, *Difference and Repetition*, 183; Gilles Deleuze, *Negotiations*, trans. Martin Joughin (New York: Columbia University Press, 1995), 44–5; and Gilles Deleuze and Félix Guattari, *A Thousand Plateaus*, trans. Brian Massumi (Minneapolis: University of Minnesota Press, 1987), 234, where Deleuze makes closely related remarks. As usual, the best and clearest summary of this concept in Deleuze's work is provided by Daniel W. Smith, *Essays on Deleuze* (Edinburgh: Edinburgh University Press, 2012), 242–5. Not only is this passage extremely helpful on its own terms, it is followed (245–7) by an explanation of the way in which Deleuze will later turn to differential calculus as a way to extend the relational model. This is arguably the real trajectory that leads from Deleuze's reading of Hume to the transcendental empiricism developed in *Difference and Repetition*, a point that we will note in passing in the next chapter.

10. As Mark Steiner points out, citing the same passages we have just seen, Kant's own account of the straight line as a synthetic

judgement repeats, almost literally, Hume's discussion. See Mark Steiner, 'Kant's Misrepresentations of Hume's Philosophy of Mathematics in the *Prolegomena*', *Hume Studies* 13:2 (1987), 400–10.

11. Immanuel Kant, *Prolegomena to Any Future Metaphysics That Will Be Able to Come Forward as Science*, trans. and ed. Gary Hatfield (Cambridge: Cambridge University Press, 2004), 20.

12. This is the third of Patricia De Martelaere's major criticisms of Deleuze in her 'Gilles Deleuze, interprète de Hume', a text I have mentioned at a number of points. The other two appear to miss the mark in certain respects. It is arguably false (as I have suggested) that Deleuze simply identifies the effects of the principles with the impressions of reflection, and the idea that that Deleuze diminishes causal association appears, on balance, to be overstating the point. Her argument that Deleuze overgeneralises the notion of relation has, however, an undeniable validity. See Patricia De Martelaere, 'Gilles Deleuze, interprète de Hume', *Revue Philosophique de Louvain* 82:54 (1984), 224–8.

13. Gilles Deleuze, *What is Grounding?*, trans. Arjen Kleinherenbrink, ed. Tony Yanick, Jason Adams and Mohammad Salemy (Grand Rapids: &&& Publishing, 2015), 5 (trans. modified).

14. Henri Bergson, *Matter and Memory*, trans. N. Paul and W. Palmer (New York, Zone Books, 1991), 135.

15. Gilles Deleuze, 'Jean Hyppolite's *Logic and Existence*', in *Desert Islands and Other Texts*, ed. David Lapoujade, trans. Michael Taormina (New York: Semiotext(e), 2004), 15.

16. Deleuze, 'Jean Hyppolite's *Logic and Existence*', 15.

17. Deleuze, 'Jean Hyppolite's *Logic and Existence*', 16.

7

A Kantian Hume

In a letter to Herder written in 1781, Hamman said of Kant: 'He certainly deserves the title, "a Prussian Hume."' No one, so far as I know, has had the temerity to state explicitly that Hume deserves the title, 'A Scottish Kant.' But almost.[1]

Thus begins Lewis White Beck's fine little text, 'A Prussian Hume and a Scottish Kant'. *Empiricism and Subjectivity* explicitly casts Kant in two roles. He appears first as the progenitor of the sceptical, epistemological reading of Hume and of empiricism, a reading that leads us into a dull cul-de-sac. This in turn induces us to gerrymander the text of the *Treatise* so severely that very little is left other than a few pages of the first book. The second Kant is one of the 'great philosophers' (ES 118/105), and an insightful critic of Hume's philosophy. This Kant 'understood the essence of associationism' (ES 123/109), and his criticisms of Hume lead us to a genuine point of difference between the two around the status of the given with respect to the principles that qualify it.

But there is a third, implicit role played by Kant in *Empiricism and Subjectivity*. Putting it most baldly, the whole of Deleuze's reading of Hume unfolds within a Kantian framework. It is not merely the case that 'Deleuze's prose teems with decidedly Kantian terminology.'[2] Nor is it even that certain interpretive gestures of *Empiricism and Subjectivity* are rein-forced with materials drawn from Kant's philosophy. A thoroughgoing Kantian orientation is evident throughout. This then is the coherent paradox of Deleuze's Hume: it disposes with the entire framework presupposed by Kant's reading of Hume only in order to advance an alternative that is profoundly Kantian in character. What he gives us is not precisely a portrait of Hume as a Scottish Kant, but rather a certain hybrid or composite: a griffon or sphinx, a binary alloy like brass or invar.

Our concern here is not to ask whether this Kantian mode of engagement is legitimate, or to ponder the degree to which this aperture on Humean thought distorts its object. This final chapter has the different and more specific task of outlining the ways in which *Empiricism and Subjectivity* is a Kantian reading of Hume.[3] But at the least we should register the fact that the ideal of bare description that seems to be identified with the history of philosophy is one that Deleuze explicitly rejects. Reams have been published on Deleuze's relationship to the history of philosophy, but in my view the illuminating parallel that John Sellars draws between Deleuze's approach and the medieval commentary tradition gets to the heart of the matter.[4] Deleuze's reading of Hume should not be expected to merely reproduce Hume's major arguments. As Sellars says,

> One does not read Proclus's commentary on Plato's *Timaeus* in order to find help when reading the *Timaeus*. Nor does one read the commentaries by Averroes, Aquinas or Duns Scotus, in order to assist one's understanding of Aristotle. To be sure, one might when reading these commentaries encounter much that will enliven one's reading of Aristotle, but that is not the principal reason why one would read them. Instead, one reads Averroes's commentaries on *De Anima*, for instance, to find his arguments concerning the unity of the intellect, and Duns Scotus's commentary on the *Metaphysics* for his theory of haecceity.[5]

Consequently, 'one should approach "Deleuze's Hume" or "Deleuze's Spinoza" in much the same way that one might approach "Proclus's Plato" or "Aquinas's Aristotle"'.[6] The situation here is, in a way, a more complicated one, since 'Deleuze's Hume' is really 'Deleuze's Kantian Hume', but the point still holds. Works in the history of philosophy are always syntheses, and when we read them this must be kept firmly in mind.

FOUR KANTIAN ELEMENTS IN EMPIRICISM AND SUBJECTIVITY

Examining *Empiricism and Subjectivity* for these Kantian elements would be a worthy task on its own terms, not least because Deleuze's later works, at least up to *Anti-Oedipus*, deploy these same elements. Here, however, we will note four significant cases of this hybridisation. But before doing this, it is worth setting aside a couple of red herrings, or rather, philosophical false friends, points at which Deleuze appears to be borrowing from Kant but where in fact the proximity is merely terminological.

The first of these is found in the phrase 'the primacy of practical reason'. It is true that both Kant and Hume argue for this primacy, even though the use of the term in relation to Hume is mine. For Hume, as we know, the realm of the practical is affective, that is, passional. Reason as it is deployed in the system of the understanding is radically subordinated to the passional order. This is to say, in more common terminology, that Hume's moral philosophy is a form of sentimentalism, and here Norman Kemp Smith was surely right to emphasise the importance of Francis Hutcheson for Hume. Like Hume, Kant very clearly thinks that theoretical reason cannot be the master of human existence. However, unlike Hume he does not restrict the ambit of rationality to epistemology, and the 'reason' in practical reason is formal, and presents us with a purely empty rule for the determination of the good. The formal emptiness and cruel inflexibility of Kant's categorical imperative (which famously leads Jacques Lacan to affiliate him with the Marquis de Sade) is absolutely anathema to Hume's practical and affective sense of the moral world. Nothing in Hume is at all compatible with Kant's famous formulation: 'So act that the maxim of your will could always hold at the same time as a principle of universal legislation.'[7]

This is just to say, conversely, that morality is and must be disjunct from any affective elements of experience for Kant. The requirement for moral agency – insofar as it expresses both our (noumenal) freedom and our rationality – is to simply 'do one's duty'. Deleuze is certainly right to invoke Kafka's famous line in this conjunction: 'the Good is what the Law says'.[8]

It is also worth noting that for Kant, it is possible for theoretical reason to maintain itself within its legitimate bounds. For Hume, however, a point that is key for Deleuze as we have seen, this is not the case. By itself, belief cannot finally distinguish between truth and fiction. It is by being grounded in something other than itself – moral life – that the excessiveness proper to the formation of belief can be moderated. But for Kant, it is of the essence that (autonomous) moral agency not be grounded in anything other than itself.

The second red herring is the category of reflection.[9] When Kant speaks of reflective judgement in the *Critique of the Power of Judgment*, he opposes it to determining judgement, the modality of judgement proper to the formation of knowledge which involves the subordination of the sensible manifold to pre-established rules (the categories of the understanding). In reflective judgement, on the other hand, there are no such rules, and a free play of the various faculties of the mind takes place. But where the Kantian subject exercises reflective judgement when making aesthetic or teleological judgements, the Humean subject is constituted as such by the mechanism of reflection. The impressions of reflection that are produced by the principles in the mind gradually activate a form of habituated subjectivity that only consequently can engage in aesthetic and epistemic judgement. And because there is no exception to the rules of habit and institution, no such 'free play' is possible.

The imagination. One of the key things that allows Deleuze to move past the epistemological reading of Hume is his emphasis on the imagination. We have seen that he will claim, for Hume, that 'empiricism is a philosophy of the imagination and not a philosophy of the senses' (ES 124/110). The passage continues in the following way:

> We know that the question 'how does the subject constitute itself within the given?' means 'how does the imagination become a faculty?' According to Hume, the imagination becomes a faculty insofar as a law of the reproduction of representations or a synthesis of reproduction is constituted as the result of principles. (ES 124/110)

It is hardly necessary to note that these texts appear right after a long citation from the first *Critique*, bearing out as strongly as they do a Kantian perspective. Now, it is true that Hume and Kant are split here by the empiricist dualism, such that the problem in Kant is not that of the constitution of the subject. The framework that Deleuze is deploying is nevertheless Kant's own. It is as though the Kantian conception of the imagination has been retrojected into the problematic of subjective constitution in Hume, so that the issue is no longer *simply* the constitution of knowledge (Hume's legitimate belief), but also the constitution of the believing subject.

Now in fact, as the 'What is Grounding?' lectures make clear, Deleuze's emphasis on the notion of the imagination is due to not just a certain Kantian emphasis found in the A edition of the first *Critique*, but to a number of other factors. In the lectures, Heidegger's reading of Kant plays an outsized role. In particular, Deleuze makes frequent reference to *Kant and the Problem of Metaphysics*, which famously makes of the imagination the element of Kant's construction in the *Critique of Pure Reason* around which everything else turns: 'everything in the essence of pure knowledge that has a synthetic structure is brought about by the imagination'.[10] Thus Heidegger writes that

> Of these three elements [intuition, imagination, understanding], the pure synthesis of the imagination holds the central position. This is not meant in a superficial sense, as if in the enumeration of the conditions of pure knowledge the imagination simply fell between the first and the third. Rather, this central position has a structural significance. In it, the pure synopsis and the pure synthesis meet and fit in with one another.[11]

Moreover, taking up the notion of transcendence itself, it is in Heidegger that we find the unity of Kant's transcendental and a subjective transcendence now transformed by phenomenology strictly speaking. We must also add to this 'the poets and writers of German Romanticism'.[12] In 'What is Grounding?' Deleuze makes particular reference to Novalis, to whom he attributes a desire to formulate a philosophy of the imagination, even a certain 'transcendental imagination'.[13] This latter displaces the old metaphysical notion of God's infinite understanding with that of the constitutive finitude of the subject. And here the imagination is no longer the means of a necessary reproduction in the service of recognition, as it is in the first *Critique*, but appears instead as creative, as productive rather than reproductive.

In sum, the point here is that Deleuze's foregrounding of the imagination in Hume draws on a series of influences that are not explicit in the text of *Empiricism and Subjectivity* itself, but which seem borne out by his slightly later work on the topic of subjectivity and transcendence. And not only do the 'What is Grounding?' lectures bear out these connections, they also show the direction in which this Kantian reading of Hume will lead Deleuze later – back through Kant and into the history of philosophy.

Space and time. The second Kantian accent is a more specific one, but it provides Deleuze with the means to institute a serious break with orthodox readings of Hume.

The standard reading of Hume on space and time emphasises their atomic character, and the problems that commonly attend our ideas of them. Now, it is true for Hume both that we have ideas of space and time (see T 1.2), and that there are relations, due to associations of contiguity and cause and effect, that are spatio-temporal in character (see, for example, T 1.2.3). But Deleuze's point here is a different one. While recognising the first of these emphases, particularly regarding space, in his discussion of the nature of bodies (ES 95–9/89–91), Deleuze takes the analysis in a strikingly Kantian direction: 'the given is not in space; the space is in the given. Space and time are in the mind' (ES 99/91). These are svelte rephrasings of Kant's famous claim in the Transcendental Aesthetic, that 'there are two pure forms of sensible intuition as principles of *a priori* cognition, namely space and time'.[14] This is to say, as Kant puts it later in the *Critique*, that 'space and time are only sensible forms of our intuition, but not determinations given for themselves, or conditions of objects as things in themselves'.[15]

Spatial and temporal features of ideas are thus more than particular relations, and the two registers must be distinguished. When Deleuze insists that 'Contiguous or distant objects do not in the least explain that distance and contiguity are *relations*' (ES 110/99), his purpose is to insist on the primacy of the relational, but the converse point also holds: certain spatial characteristics of objects belong to the mind without being produced in it by the principles of association. Here is the Kantian kernel of Deleuze's treatment of space and time in *Empiricism and Subjectivity*.

Earlier I noted the ubiquity in Hume scholarship of the idea that Hume distinguishes between matters of fact and the products of demonstrative reasoning by claiming the latter gives us analytic truths – that is, truths that belong to ideas prior to their association by relation. Particularly strong evidence for this reading is found in geometrical reasoning, where spatial relations appear to be given directly in ideas like 'the shortest line', but, as we have seen, Deleuze advances a strong argument to the effect that this confuses relationality (product of the principles) and spatiality (formal characteristic belonging to all impressions arising from sight and touch).

This might seem to be a rather specific point to highlight, but for the fact that what is at stake in making of space and time forms of intuition is the empiricist claim *par excellence* for Deleuze that 'relations are external to their terms'. If demonstrative reason turns around analytic truths, then this claim has a restricted range – it would pertain only to matters of fact – and its primacy would be vitiated. Deleuze's recourse to Kantian concepts allows him to maintain a key part of his reconstruction of Hume and construction of a definition of empiricism.

Transcendental illusion. But now we arrive at the most important Kantian element in *Empiricism and Subjectivity*, one that plays an outsized role in the composition of Deleuze's reading of Hume. In his 1972 summary of Hume's philosophy, Deleuze writes that

> for the traditional concept of error [Hume] substitutes the concept of illusion or delirium, according to which there are not false but illegitimate beliefs, illegitimate operations of the faculties, and the illegitimate functioning of relations. In this respect, Kant once again owes something essential to Hume. We're not threatened by error. It's much worse: we're swimming in delirium.[16]

And in 1991, Deleuze will write in the English preface of *Empiricism and Subjectivity* that 'Illegitimate beliefs perhaps inevitably surround thought like a cloud of illusions. In this respect, Hume anticipates Kant' (ES ix). But when we examine the text of *Empiricism and Subjectivity* itself, it seems rather that, in explaining the place of uncorrectable fictions in Hume's system, and even this very category itself, Deleuze is freely drawing from Kant's analysis of transcendental illusion.[17]

We have already seen the fourfold analysis on this point. While reason provides us with a way to reflectively weigh the likelihood of particular beliefs, there are some that we find ourselves unable to correct in any way: beliefs in the world (or the totality), God (as the cause of the principles themselves), and the persistence of objects (as the cause of experience itself). Not only do these ideas arise within us as pure fictions, we find that we presuppose them in even the most anodyne acts of belief. Worse again is the fact that we discover the operation of fiction at the very root of experience – it is a principle of human nature itself.

Like Kant, Deleuze's Hume argues that not only does the mind's grasp on the world have an absolute limit, but the very act of grasping, and indeed the hand with which we grasp, are compromised by fictions – in belief, madness and delusion reign.

Other than the various ramifications of the empiricist dualism – which we can register simply by saying that Kant is a transcendental thinker – the sole difference between Kant and Deleuze's Hume on this point is that the fictions of persistent objecthood, the world and God can have no non-parasitic function for the latter.[18] That there is no regulative use of these fictions is in part because the opposition between constitutive and regulative is split between the principles on the one hand, and general rules on the other, which are unique elements in the system of the self. But it is more important to note that, as fictions, they can never contribute anything at all to beliefs. It is true that, should we push the analysis of the origin of belief back far enough, we find ourselves confronted by them, and by the ur-fiction of objecthood. But this shows us nothing about what systematically organises beliefs, only the absolute limit of human thought. The damage to the possibility of knowledge is absolute: we have 'no choice left but betwixt a false reason and none at all' (T 1.4.7.7).

Our sole recourse, as we know, is intersubjective life, which does not correct but modulates the fictions of belief: 'The illusion of the fancy is the reality of culture. The reality of culture is an illusion from the point of view of the understanding, but it asserts itself within a domain where the understanding can not, and should not, seek to dissipate illusion' (ES 56/62).

Purposiveness. The final point concerns the problem of the relationship between being and human being, nature and human nature: the idea of purposiveness. It is true, as we have already seen, that Hume explicitly invokes a pre-established harmony

157

between these two poles in the first *Enquiry*. Beyond this, though, and even taking into account the discussion of 'purpose' in the *Dialogues concerning Natural Religion*, Deleuze's introduction of the problem of purposiveness into his reading of Hume is striking, to say the least.[19]

In fact, the concept is really developed for the first time by Kant in the *Critique of the Power of Judgment*. In the so-called First Introduction, Kant will write that 'purposiveness is a lawfulness of the contingent as such'.[20] It provides us with a representation of being as a being ordered such that we can enter into certain kinds of relationship with it. It is, in other words, the principle of a certain regulated relationship between being as it is in itself and subjectivity. Here is Kant:

> This transcendental concept of a purposiveness of nature is neither a concept of nature nor a concept of freedom, since it attributes nothing at all to the object (of nature), but rather only represents the unique way in which we must proceed in reflection on the objects of nature with the aim of a thoroughly interconnected experience, consequently it is a subjective principle (maxim) of the power of judgment.[21]

Aside from this invocation of the transcendental, there is nothing here that would be out of place in *Empiricism and Subjectivity*. At the same time, little of this would find a comfortable place in the *Treatise* or even the less severe *Enquiry*.

Nevertheless, the concept of purposiveness plays a central role in Deleuze's reading of Hume. We do know that the problem of purposiveness, or rather the problem of its status, is resolved at the very end of the book by sublating it to the ongoing adventure of social life, and in particular to the activity of philosophy itself. And here, it would appear that Deleuze and Kant part ways, since – as the citation above indicates – neither theoretical nor practical reason, concept of nature nor concept of freedom are at stake in it. But this perspective itself is overturned by Deleuze in his little book on Kant. In fact, the conclusion of *Kant's Critical Philosophy* and the final pages of *Empiricism and Subjectivity* make essentially the same point around the relationship between purposiveness and the practical life of the subject, grounding the former in the latter. Deleuze writes that:

> The essential point is that the *Critique of Judgment* gives us a new theory of finality, which corresponds to the transcendental point of view and fits perfectly with the idea of legislation. This task is fulfilled in so far *as finality no longer has a theological principle, but rather, theology has a 'final' human foundation.* From this derives the importance of the two theses of the *Critique of Judgment:* that the final accord of the faculties is the object of a special genesis; and that the final relationship between Nature and man is the result of a *human* practical activity.[22]

Once again, this line of analysis replays – in Deleuze's own inimitable way, of course – the structure of Heidegger's *Kant and the Problem of Metaphysics*, with its turn to the problem of anthropology at the end. The only real difference is that in the Kant book, Deleuze is explicit in marking the problem of purposiveness as a troubling residual of uncritical philosophy. There are three years between *Empiricism and Subjectivity* and the assertion, in the 'What is Grounding?' lectures, that Hume's use of the thematic of pre-established harmony 'remains disquieting on the part of an author who attacks the idea of God'.[23] Between the discussion of purposiveness in the third *Critique* and the question whether Kant is not 'simply reintroducing the idea of harmony and finality?'[24] in Deleuze's book on Kant there are three pages.

AN UNTIMELY HUME

After the publication of *Empiricism and Subjectivity*, Deleuze's own philosophy develops by exploding and reassembling Kant's transcendental philosophy with materials found in Kant's precursors (Hume, but also Spinoza and Leibniz), in Kant's critics (Maimon, Hegel and Heidegger) and Deleuze's near-contemporaries (Simondon, Ruyer, Lautman, and so on).

The apparition of a properly idiosyncratic and radical Hume that Deleuze's first book presents wavers and then vanishes. In the 'What is Grounding?' lectures, and while he is hailed as the one who 'stumbled onto an extraordinary problem',[25] the problem of the grounds of knowledge, he appears as a figure clearly and completely surpassed by Kant, Hegel and Heidegger. In *Difference and Repetition*, published in 1968, Hume is summoned to make a single point, and one also made more forcefully by Bergson and Freud.[26]

At the same time, it would certainly be a mistake to completely subordinate the Hume of *Empiricism and Subjectivity* to Deleuze's own philosophical project, one that arguably comes to fullest flower in *Difference and Repetition* and *The Logic of Sense*. Tracing the development of these mature works is an essential part of Deleuze scholarship, of course, and a fecund means for grasping their sense. But – and this is the essential point of the current book – we can also read *Empiricism and Subjectivity* on its own terms, and try to grasp its internal structure.

The history of philosophy is perhaps poorly named, since the goal is not to assemble a progressive trajectory of accumulated achievements, as if philosophy were a science. Ironically, it is those philosophers who most stridently pursue this identification – and who define philosophical progress in scientific terms – that at once reject the significance of philosophy's past and, in endorsing the notion of progress, cling most strongly to the core doctrines of a certain patent image of history. Such intellects are without a doubt the Whigs of contemporary philosophy.

As Alain Badiou likes to say, the great philosophers are our perennial contemporaries. Consequently, the history of philosophy can only attain its highest point when it dispenses with history altogether, and presents a philosopher as an idiosyncratic singularity, a perennial aberration, a 'strange uncouth monster' (T 1.4.7.2). *Empiricism and Subjectivity* gives Hume back to us in just this way

NOTES

1. Lewis White Beck, 'A Prussian Hume and a Scottish Kant', in *Essays on Kant and Hume* (New Haven, CT: Yale University Press, 1978), 111.

2. Peter S. Fosl, 'Empiricism, Difference, and Common Life', *Man and World* 26:3, 324.

3. The comparative reading of *Empiricism and Subjectivity* and *Kant's Critical Philosophy* would also be revealing here, and while I will occasionally refer to it in what follows, it is not something that will be seriously pursued. Readers interested in this conjunction have probably already had cause to examine the most useful texts on the matter found in Christian Kerslake's *Immanence and the Vertigo of Philosophy: From Kant to Deleuze* (Edinburgh: Edinburgh University Press, 2009).

4. John Sellars, 'Deleuze and the History of Philosophy', *British Journal for the History of Philosophy* 15:3 (2007), 551–60.

5. Sellars, 'Deleuze and the History of Philosophy', 559–60.

6. Sellars, 'Deleuze and the History of Philosophy', 560.

7. Immanuel Kant, *Critique of Practical Reason*, trans. Werner Pluhar (Indianapolis: Hackett Publishing, 2002), 45.

8. Gilles Deleuze, *Kant's Critical Philosophy*, trans. Hugh Tomlinson and Barbara Habberjam (London: Athlone, 1984), x.

9. On this, see Fosl, 'Empiricism, Difference, and Common Life', 324.

10. Martin Heidegger, *Kant and the Problem of Metaphysics*, 5th edn, trans. Richard Taft (Indianapolis: Indiana University Press, 1997), 66.

11. Heidegger, *Kant and the Problem of Metaphysics*, 45. This text of Heidegger's recalls the following remark in *Empiricism and Subjectivity*: 'Kant, of course, does not doubt that the imagination is effectively the best possible terrain for raising the problem of knowledge. Of the three syntheses that he distinguishes, he himself presents the synthesis of the imagination as the foundation of the other two' (ES 124/110–11). And indeed, since the three syntheses (apprehension, reproduction, recognition; see Immanuel Kant, *Critique of Pure Reason*, trans. and ed. Paul Guyer and Allen W. Wood (Cambridge: Cambridge University Press, 1997), A120) belong to intuition, imagination and the understanding, the two are making essentially the same point.

12. Gilles Deleuze, *What is Grounding?*, trans. Arjen Kleinheren-brink, ed. Tony Yanick, Jason Adams and Mohammad Salemy (Grand Rapids: &&& Publishing, 2015), 168.

13. Deleuze, *What is Grounding?*, 168.

14. Kant, *Critique of Pure Reason*, A22/B36.

15. Kant, *Critique of Pure Reason*, A369.

16. Gilles Deleuze, 'Hume', in *Desert Islands and Other Texts*, ed. David Lapoujade, trans. Michael Taormina (New York: Semiotext(e), 2004), 165.

17. See Peter Thielke's excellent analysis of the parallels between Hume and Kant on this score: 'Hume, Kant and the Sea of Illusion', *Hume Studies* 29:1 (2003), 63–88. The strength of this analysis, in my view, is the means it provides Thielke to limit the reach of the naturalist reading of Hume (at least insofar as we are dealing with his supposed naturalist epistemology). However, to the degree that he remains within a broadly epistemological framework, the only capacity to redress the illusory character of experience is found 'in the fact that the exposure of the illusions that beset the imagination can itself provide a bit of solace' (83). But this is to neglect the sphere of the social. On the importance for Deleuze of the category of transcendental illusion, see Jon Roffe, 'Error, Illusion, Deception: Deleuze against James', in *Deleuze and Pragmatism*, ed. Sean Bowden and Simone Bignall (London: Routledge, 2014), 73–88.

18. As Thielke puts it, 'where Kant's transcendental idealism claims to find a corrective to these errors, Hume [. . .] finds no such safe haven' (Thielke, 'Hume, Kant and the Sea of Illusion', 63).

19. I agree with Christian Kerslake when he writes that 'Almost all of Deleuze's works up to *Difference and Repetition* affirm purposiveness as the final tribunal for the coherence of a system' (Kerslake, *Immanence and the Vertigo of Philosophy*, 103). His analyses of this topic, to my knowledge the only substantial contribution, are well worth examining.

20. Immanuel Kant, *Critique of the Power of Judgment*, ed. Paul Guyer, trans. Paul Guyer and Eric Matthews (Cambridge: Cambridge University Press, 2002), 20:217; 20.

21. Kant, *Critique of the Power of Judgment*, 5:184; 71.

22. Deleuze, *Kant's Critical Philosophy*, 69.

23. Deleuze, *What is Grounding?*, 5.
24. Deleuze, *Kant's Critical Philosophy*, 69.
25. Deleuze, *What is Grounding?*, 26.
26. Interestingly, when Bergson and Freud are summoned together in *Empiricism and Subjectivity*, it is in order to claim that Hume had already anticipated their way of prioritising habitual association over psychic atomism (ES 114–15/102–3): 'The least we can say', Deleuze writes here, 'is that Hume thought of it first' (ES 114/103). In *Difference and Repetition*, where the historical sequence of philosophical inventions is roundly ignored in the name of philosophy itself, Hume's account appears as merely propaedeutic.

Index

Descartes, René, 8, 89
desire, 40, 41, 60, 71, 110
  sexual, 78n, 122
*Dialogues concerning Natural
  Religion*, xiii, 96, 158
Difference and Repetition,
  121, 131, 147n, 160,
  162n, 163n
drives, 48, 59, 60, 77n; *see
  also* tendencies
dualism *see* empiricist dualism
During, Elie, 117

effects, 5, 10, 51
  of belief, 27, 29
  of the passions, 40, 44
  of the principles, 13–14,
    21–2, 24–5, 42, 59, 91,
    110, 113, 116, 122, 126n,
    127n, 148n
  see also passions, the;
    principle(s) of association
egoism/egotist, 13, 46–7
Einstein, Albert, 2
emotions, 40, 42, 74, 115; *see
  also* passions, the
empiricism, xi , xiii, 5–6, 9,
  11, 98, 100, 107, 114,
  117–19, 125, 129–30,
  132–6, 139–45, 147n,
  149, 153, 156–7
*Empiricism and Subjectivity:
  An Essay on Hume's
  Theory of Human Nature*,

xi, xii–xiv, 5, 7, 10, 14,
  16n, 19, 24–5, 27, 34,
  36n, 38, 43, 50, 75n, 76n,
  77n, 81, 84, 96, 98, 100,
  103, 104–5, 109, 113,
  115, 117–18, 127n, 128n,
  129, 135, 140–5, 146n,
  149–51, 154–6, 158–60,
  161n, 163n
empiricist dualism, 107,
  134–6, 139–41, 143, 145,
  153, 157
*Enquiry concerning Human
  Understanding, An*, 12,
  17n, 28–9, 96, 136, 158
*Enquiry concerning the
  Principles of Morals, An*,
  xiii, 39, 44
*Essay on the Nature and
  Immutability of Truth*, 4
experience, 2–3, 4, 5, 6, 7–8,
  11, 12, 16n, 17n, 19, 22,
  24, 26–31, 32, 39, 43–5,
  46, 53, 55, 60, 72, 74, 82,
  83, 85, 86–7, 90, 92–5, 96,
  97–8, 99, 106–8, 114, 119,
  120–1, 132–3, 136, 137–9,
  152, 156–7, 158, 162n
  as a principle of human
    nature, 14, 133
  see also habit; ideas;
    impressions
experimental reason *see*
  reason

A quarterly forum for new work on the writings of Gilles Deleuze, **Deleuze Studies** does not limit itself to any one field: it is neither a philosophy journal, nor a literature journal, nor a cultural studies journal, but all three and more.

www.euppublishing.com/loi/dls

EDITOR: Ian Buchanan, University of Wollongong
EXECUTIVE EDITOR: David Savat, University of Western Australia
ART EDITOR: Andrea Eckersley, Monash University
REVIEWS EDITOR: Ian Buchanan, University of Wollongong